Exploring the World

of COLMCILLE

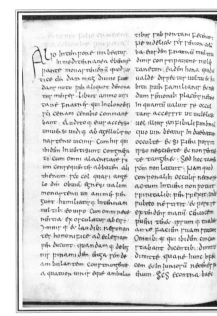

also known as COLUMBA

MAIRÉAD ASHE FITZGERALD was born in the parish of Colmcille in County Longford and grew up in Clare. A former teacher of Irish and history, she currently works in a Dublin publishing house. In recent years she studied archaeology at University College, Dublin.

'Beautifully produced and written. This is a book to keep, and one which will be enjoyed by readers young and old; a nice reminder of the glory of our early church, and of the life of a remarkable man.'
Leinster Leader

'Reveals a complex and charismatic character ... we also get a fascinating picture of life and politics in sixth century Ireland.'
Clare Champion

'An attractive and very readable account of Colmcille and his world.'
Archaeology Ireland

'Written in an accessible style, with plenty of detailed facts for the curious.'
Children's Books in Ireland

'A fascinating book.'
Southside People

Exploring The World of
Colmcille

also known as
Columba

MAIRÉAD ASHE FITZGERALD

Illustrated by Stephen Hall

THE O'BRIEN PRESS
DUBLIN

This edition first published 2000 by The O'Brien Press Ltd.,
20 Victoria Road, Rathgar, Dublin 6, Ireland.
Tel: +353 1 4923333; Fax: +353 1 4922777
E-mail books@obrien.ie
Website www.obrien.ie
First published in hardback in 1997.

ISBN: 0-86278-665-7

British Library Cataloguing-in-Publication Data
FitzGerald, Mairéad
The world of Colmcille also known as Columba
1 Columba, Saint, of Iona 2. Christian saints – biography
I. Title II. Hall, Stephen
270'.092

3 4 5 6 7 8 9 10
00 01 02 03 04 05 06

Typesetting, layout, editing, design: The O'Brien Press Ltd.
Colour separations: C&A Print Services Ltd.
Printing: MPG Ltd.

THE PHOTOGRAPHS
The author and publisher thank the following for photographs: Stadtbibliothek
Schaffhausen (Switzerland), Msc. Gen. 1 for page 1; Professor Michael Herity 28,
57; the National Museum of Ireland 14, 33, 85; The Board of Trinity College Dublin
87, 89; Royal Irish Academy 83, 84, back cover; Crown Copyright, reproduced by
Permission of Historic Scotland 72, 73; Dept. Of Arts, Culture & the Gaeltacht,
Heritage Services 16, 18, 21, 23, 99; Cambridge University Collection 15; Shannon
Development 17; Des Lavelle 22; Bord Fáilte 37; the illustration on page 69 is by
David Rooney from *Exploring the Book of Kells*; photos on pages 13, 55 are the
author's own.
MAPS: Lynn Pierce.

BACK COVER
Initial letter from the Cathach folio 48R, courtesy Royal Irish Academy.

ILLUSTRATION ON PAGE 1
This is an extract from Adomnán's Vita Columbae. Adomnán's own manuscript is
no longer in existence and this extract is from a copy of it made in Iona by a monk
called Dorbene, who died in AD 713. The manuscript was taken to Germany to
escape the Viking invasions, and is now in a library in Switzerland.

 CONTENTS

DEDICATION

Do m'athair, Mícheál Ághas (1915-1992),

i ndilchuimhne

ACKNOWLEDGEMENTS

In researching the material for this book, I have drawn on the resources of many people, places, books and institutions. Like anyone who has made a study of Colmcille and his world, Adomnán's Vita Columbae is the book I am most indebted to. It is a never-failing resource that one turns to repeatedly for the insights it provides into life so many centuries ago, but most of all for the living accounts it gives of life in an Early Christian monastery. I have listed this work in two editions along with many of the other valuable books related to this subject in the Bibliography at the back of the book.

Many people were helpful to me and made gathering the material for the book such a fascinating adventure. I have my friend Ena Fair to thank for encouraging me to write in the first place. My friends and colleagues at The O'Brien Press were so supportive and helpful that it convinced me to see it through. To them all, my sincere thanks, especially Michael, Íde and Lynn. My sons Fergus and Eoghan patiently allowed themselves to be persuaded to try out the work-in-progress and they made valuable suggestions to me from their youthful perspective. My husband Deasmhumhain kept me supplied with a steady stream of books. I owe my sincere thanks to my cousins Fionnuala and Colm Geary in Derry. Their friendship and generosity enhanced my knowledge of and appreciation for that historic city.

In Colmcille's native Gartan in County Donegal I was privileged to have as my guide Mr Gerald Columba Doherty who gave me the benefit of his knowledge of the local lore of Colmcille. My thanks to him and to his wife Alice. Thanks too to the many people I encountered in Iona, especially Mr and Mrs Morison.

I owe my thanks to the staff of the Department of Irish Folklore in University College Dublin for permission to consult the material on Colmcille in their archives.

An Outline of the Events of Colmcille's Life

◎ He was born in Gartan in Donegal in AD 521 into the ruling tribal dynasty of the Uí Néill (O'Neills).

◎ Brought up a Christian and educated in various monastic schools such as that of Saint Finnian of Moville; in Clonard with another Finnian; in Glasnevin with Saint Mobhí.

◎ He founded monasteries in Ireland before his famous exile in Iona (563). Legend has it that he left because of a self-imposed penance, having caused a battle over a copy of a book of Saint Finnian's.

◎ His other purpose in settling in Iona was to convert the pagan Picts of Scotland.

◎ He was a person of great influence with kings and chieftains in Ireland and Scotland.

◎ He is important most of all for the learning that he passed on to generations of scribes and scholars who followed him. His influence was lasting, as off-shoots of Iona sprang up over Scotland and Northumbria, and the learning which he brought to Iona was to spread far and wide over Scotland and England.

◎ He returned to Ireland at least once, to attend the great Convention of Druim Ceatt.

◎ He died in Iona in 597.

Map showing places mentioned in the text.

CHAPTER ONE

Colmcille's Early Life

Before Colmcille was born in AD 521 in present-day County Donegal his mother, the young princess Eithne, had a dream. In the dream, a magnificent and beautiful cloak was given to her by an angel. It was covered in flowers of every imaginable colour and all the perfumes of the flowers filled the air around it. Much to her sorrow the cloak was carried away up into the sky, but it grew and spread until it covered all of Ireland and Scotland. Eithne was much consoled when the angel told her that the dream meant that the son who was about to be born to her was going to have a remarkable influence and would spread the Christian faith and learning all over the lands of Ireland and Scotland.

With such delightful legends as this, people in Early Christian and Medieval times embroidered the facts about the saints they loved (holy men and women became what we may call folk-saints, known in stories and traditions as 'saints'). They did this in order to commemorate and make special the memories of these beloved people, much as they took special care of objects such as books which may have belonged to them and dressed up these mementos in beautiful containers with jewels and ornate metalwork. Colmcille, as the dream in the legend foretold, did indeed grow up to lead a remarkable life.

Like Saint Patrick, he's one of the best-known and best-loved of our early Irish saints, but, unlike Patrick he was a native Irish person, a prince, in fact, only four generations removed from Niall of the Nine Hostages, his great-great-grandfather, who was famous for stealing slaves from across the Irish Sea. In fact, one of the most interesting things about Colmcille is the way in which his life connected that old pagan Celtic world to the new order that came with Christianity. Furthermore, he was at the beginning of the great exodus of Irish scholars which was to bring learning and spirituality to Western Europe during the Dark Ages, and to foster the arts in the form of book illumination and calligraphy.

Colmcille himself and the events of his life are full of interesting contrasts. He knew the world of the pagan past and became a priest of the new religion himself. He is popularly seen as a holy man who founded monasteries and wrote books, but there was much more to him than this. He had a deep understanding of the politics of his day and was often called on by kings and chieftains to intervene in their disputes. The poets too looked on him as their champion. He was a person of great influence and vision, interesting for the sheer force of his personality. He was headstrong and fiery, but on the other hand he was gentle and spiritual. His remarkable personality caused numerous legends to grow up around him in his lifetime and keep his memory alive.

His cousin, Adomnán, who was abbot of Colmcille's famous monastery in Iona a century after Colmcille's death, wrote an account of his life while memories of him were still fresh in people's minds. Adomnán's book, the Vita Columbae, was only the beginning. Legends and tales about his life, his sayings and his prophecies continued to grow and circulate all through the Middle Ages. Churches and monasteries founded long after his death were dedicated to him. Books and poems connected with him have exercised the minds of scholars for generations. In 1535 Manus O'Donnell, a chieftain of Donegal and one of Colmcille's descendants, made another great collection of all that was known about him in a book called Betha Colaim Cille. Again, in this century, when folklore was being collected and written down all over Irleand, there were more legends collected about Colmcille than about any other Irish saint. They are recorded in the Department of Irish Folklore in University College Dublin. The events of Colmcille's life are written about too in various annals such as the Annals of Ulster. These are historical accounts, usually written in monasteries, of events that really happened. They are our earliest sources of historical events (see Chapter 10).

Fourteen hundred years later we are urged to ask what was the real story of this remarkable person and what do the events of his life tell us about the very different world he and his contemporaries lived in so long ago?

EARLY LIFE

For the times that he lived in, Colmcille's life was remarkable from the beginning. He was born in Gartan in Donegal in the year 521 where he has an unrivalled place in the folk-memory to this day. He was a prince of the most powerful dynasty in the Ireland of his day, the Northern Uí Néill (O'Neills). His mother, Eithne, was a princess from a ruling tribe in Leinster. His father was Fedelmidh, a great-grandson of Niall of the Nine Hostages, one of the last great pagan kings of Celtic times who, in one of his raids on the west coast of Britain, brought home the young Patrick, the same Patrick who was to bring the Christian faith to Ireland. So, though Ireland may have been Christianised, it was still very close to its pagan past when Colmcille was a boy.

Ancient cross in Gartan graveyard in Co. Donegal close to the place where Colmcille was born in 521.

His family belonged to the Cenél Chonaill, a branch of the Northern Uí Néill. They were the overlords of present-day Tír Chonaill (County Donegal). Another branch of the family was the Cenél Eoghain, who gave their name to Inishowen in Donegal, and later to modern Tír Eoghain (County Tyrone).

Gartan, where Colmcille was born, is a large rural parish today in a magnificent landscape of lakes and mountains.

Customs, memories and legends about the saint are part of the rich folklore of the place. According to tradition, he was

born at Leac na Cumha, which means 'the flagstone of the sorrows', and the very flagstone where he is believed to have been born is pointed out by the local people in the townland, also called Leac na Cumha, overlooking Gartan Lough.

At birth, Colmcille was named Crimhthann, which means 'fox', and was bap-

A cast bronze bell from Gartan, dating from the eighth century AD.

tised at Tulach Dubhghlaise (Temple-douglas). Like many young princes, according to the old Celtic custom in Ireland, he was sent for fosterage (*ar altromas* is the traditional Irish term) away from home. The sons of kings and chieftains, according to the old Celtic custom, were often sent to be raised in the household of another chieftain, usually for the purpose of forging friendly alliances or for education. Thus Colmcille spent some years of his youth in the household of a holy man called Cruithnechan. Cruithnechan lived in Doire Eithne, which is the area around modern Kilmacrenan, eight miles away from Gartan Lough through the valley of the river Lennan.

Ireland in Colmcille's day was rural and agricultural. Unlike other European countries, there were no towns or cities, and most people lived in protected farmsteads known as ringforts. You can see the remains of these ringforts in nearly every townland in Ireland today, and locals generally refer to them as the *lios* or 'fairy fort'. There are traces of almost fifty thousand of them around the country still.

A ringfort is a circular earth and stone enclosure measuring about thirty feet across, with one entrance. The houses within the ringforts, being built of wood, have disappeared, but we know that they were generally round in shape, built of wattle and daub, with a thatched roof. This is where the

Lismore Fort, a ringfort or 'lios' in Co. Louth.
People lived in circular houses for protection within ringforts like this one in Early Christian Ireland.

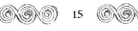

farming family lived, surrounded by their fields and crops. We can imagine the cattle and sheep being driven into them at night to keep them safe from wild animals and robbers. In Donegal, about two hundred ringforts survive today, and about the same number of cashels, which are stone versions of the ringforts.

The most spectacular of these is the Grianán of Aileach, which was the stronghold of one branch of Colmcille's fam-

The Grianán of Aileach, west of Derry,
stronghold of one branch of the Northern Uí Néill,
the dynasty to which Colmcille belonged.

ily. It's a great landmark today, situated as it is in an ancient enclosure overlooking Lough Foyle and Lough Swilly, commanding the countryside in all directions.

Reconstruction of a crannóg *at Craggaunowen, Co. Clare.*

Sometimes people lived in *crannógs*, which are artificial islands built in lakes. These were made by assembling a platform of stones and timber to form a little island where the family built their house. The tiny island known as Gallagher's Isle in Gartan Lake is thought to be a *crannóg*, but it can be difficult to tell a *crannóg* from a real island just by looking at it.

Even though these farmsteads, in ringforts, cashels and *crannog*s, may have been far apart from each other, there were very strong ties between each family and the other families of the tribe (or *tuath*). Each tribe had its own king or *rí tuaithe* who acted as protector of his people. The people, in turn, were expected to do battle for the king in his struggles with his neighbouring kings and chieftains. Indeed, battles were the order of the day.

There were about one hundred and fifty kingdoms in

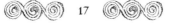

Ireland in Colmcille's day, each king ruling over his own *tuath* or tribe and each engaged in power-struggles with his neighbours. Each of these kings in turn was ruled by an over-king, with a *rí cúige* ruling a province. (The Irish word *cúige*, meaning 'province', literally means 'a fifth' because there were originally five provinces in Ireland. They became seven sometime during the centuries of Early Christian times, yet the name *cúige* remained as it does to this day.) Over them all was the *ard rí* who ruled from Tara, although in reality no *ard rí* ruled over the whole of Ireland. It was this powerful position as high king that was occupied on and off for centuries by the Northern Uí Néill, the dynasty to which Colmcille belonged. Indeed, Colmcille could well have become *ard rí* had

Tara, Co. Meath, the most famous royal site in Ireland.

he not become a monk, and throughout his life he was to be involved in the affairs of kings. During his long life, he was renowned as a great arbitrator and diplomat, and was often called on in troubled times to bring peace between rulers.

However, despite their deeply entrenched pagan way of life and the delight they took in warfare, the Irish had welcomed Christianity into their hearts by the time of Colmcille's birth, and Colmcille was a deeply committed Christian from the start. From his early boyhood, Colmcille displayed the strength of character and the single-mindedness for which he was to be famous in later life. His devotion to the Christian way of life was remarkable and caused him to spend long hours praying and meditating in the church. His friends and family respected his devotion and, thinking that Crimhthann was an unsuitable pagan name for him, they began to call him Colmcille, which means 'dove of the church', Columba in the Latin.

CHAPTER TWO

The Education of a Young Christian Prince

For his education Colmcille travelled far from Donegal, first to Moville at the head of Strangford Lough where he was a pupil of Saint Finnian. Next he went south to Leinster where he spent some time with Gemman, an aged bard. Then he moved to the renowned monastic school at Clonard in present-day County Meath where another Saint Finnian was abbot. Saint Patrick had founded the church at Clonard and it later became a famous monastic school under this Saint Finnian, who had spent years studying in Wales.

EARLY IRISH MONASTERIES

Ireland was dotted with monasteries during Colmcille's lifetime. (These Early Christian monasteries or hermitages must not be confused with the later monastic foundations of orders such as the Cistercians and the Augustinians who built great medieval abbeys after the arrival of the Normans in the twelfth century.) The Church that Saint Patrick had brought to Ireland was probably diocesan, that is, organised with bishops in charge of dioceses. But this ordered Roman way of doing things was quickly abandoned by the Irish. They preferred to live in tiny communities of monks with a holy man

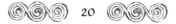

as abbot, living lives of hardship and penance as the Desert Fathers did. These Desert Fathers were people like Saint Paul (not the Saint Paul of the Bible) and Saint Anthony who went into the great deserts of Egypt to live lives of extreme hardship, fasting and prayer in order to forget all about the world and concentrate totally on the greatness of God. Many Irishmen in the fifth century learned of this way of living when they studied in monasteries like Candida Casa in Scotland and Mynyw in Wales. When they came back to Ireland they founded their own monasteries in the nearest thing to a desert that they could find – in the middle of huge bogs, or on tiny islands in rivers or off the wild west coast. Many Irish placenames with the element *díseart* (*desertum* in Latin) tell us today that at one time a tiny community lived in such a place with a holy man as abbot.

A panel from the great high cross at Moone, Co. Kildare depicting St Paul and St Anthony breaking bread in the desert after a long fast.

Beehive huts in the monastery of Sceilg Mhichíl off the coast of Kerry.
There is a further settlement on the south peak of the rocky island at a dizzying height of 218m.

You can still see the remains of many of these little hermitages today on windswept islands off the west coast because they were built of stone (though the very earliest of them were often built of wood, as archaeologists have found). The ruins of little stone monasteries are still standing in islands like Inishmurray and Inishkea North, both of which are associated with Colmcille. On High Island and Omey Island off the coast of Galway there are the ruins of tiny hermitages founded by Saint Feichín. Further to the south, some forgotten little community lived on Bishop's Island, off the stormy cliffs of the coast of Clare. But the most spectacular of them all (and maybe later than Colmcille's time) must be the settlement clinging to the craggy surface of Sceilg Mhichíl, a rocky island off the coast of Kerry.

Life in these isolated hermitages must have been gruellingly hard, 'on the very edge of the known world'. They were nearly all alike, with a tiny church or prayer-house, and they usually had a little slab with a simple cross, as well as the tomb of the founder saint. A small distance away were the circular cells or sleeping-houses of the monks. They survived only because they were built of stone, but all across Ireland there were hundreds of these monastic settlements built of wood and long since vanished. What we see today in Clonmacnoise and Glendalough are later stone buildings of the extended monasteries which grew on the sites of the earlier wooden ones. High crosses and round towers came centuries later.

Women were equally attracted to the monastic way of life and lived in nunneries, but many of these would have disappeared after the death of the foundress because according to Irish law a woman could inherit land for life only and after her death it would revert to the tribe or *tuath*. But Saint Brighid's great

An Ogham stone at Kilmalkedar, Co. Kerry.

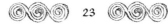

monastery in Kildare for both women and men survived for centuries, as did Saint Moninne's at Kileevy on Slieve Gullion in County Armagh; and in County Limerick, Saint Íde had a nunnery at Kileedy.

But not all monasteries were hermitages given over to fasting and prayer. Some became great monastic schools with hundreds of scholars flocking to them because they became famous for their learning.

In old pagan Ireland, up to a century before the time of Colmcille, no-one could read or write, even though the Irish were very learned. Their script, known as Ogham, was suitable only for carving on stones and the learned men – the poets, the historians and the law-makers (or Brehons) – had memorised all they knew and taught their students to learn everything by heart. But when Saint Patrick came, bringing a whole new Christian culture with knowledge in books, the Irish took to it wholeheartedly, setting up schools, learning Latin, copying manuscripts.

Monasteries like Clonmacnoise, Clonard, Glendalough, Glasnevin were famous schools in Colmcille's lifetime. It was to Saint Mobhí's school in Glasnevin in Dublin that Colmcille went when he left Clonard. One of the legends collected in the sixteenth century by Manus O'Donnell tells us that there were fifty students studying with the abbot Mobhí at that time; their cells were on the west side of the river Fionnglas, and the church was on the eastern bank. When the river was in flood one morning, Colmcille was the only student brave

enough to swim across for the morning prayers. Mobhí welcomed him like a hero, extolling his remarkable courage and strength, declaring that only the noble son of Cenél Chonaill would dare to attempt to get across and that the special protection of God looked after this chosen son. When it was time for the return journey, Colmcille was favoured with a great miracle – the students' cells were found to be transported to the church side of the river, saving him from another dangerous journey home!

But his time in Glasnevin was cut short by the arrival of a plague called the *Buidhe Chonaill* which was devastating the country, Leinster in particular. Mobhí had to send his students back to their homes for their own safety. This terrible plague had come from Europe. It began in Egypt around 540 and was carried to Ireland on ships from the Continent. Some historians believe that the contact between the Church in France and in Ireland may have helped to spread this plague.

Colmcille was ordained a priest but never became a bishop. He was an abbot, a ruler of monasteries instead, with many monasteries in his *paruchia*, or monastic family. From Glasnevin, he set out for Donegal and he and his companions did escape the plague. He had promised Saint Mobhí that he would wait for his permission before establishing his first monastery. Mobhí died in 545, a victim of the plague, and it was then that Colmcille set about his work as a founder of monasteries.

CHAPTER THREE

Founder of Monasteries

DERRY OF THE OAK-WOODS

Of all the places linked with Colmcille – apart from Iona – Derry is believed to be the one closest to his heart, and it's true to say that to this day, Colmcille is one of the most well-loved people ever associated with this historic place. Schools, streets, churches and people carry his name in its various forms: Colmcille, Columb, Colm, Columba. His feast-day is celebrated on the ninth of June each year when people wear the oak leaf to commemorate him.

It was already an important place. One of Colmcille's relatives, a chieftain of the Cenél Chonaill, had his stronghold here on the banks of the river Foyle within sight of the Grianán of Aileach. The place was known as Daire Calgach and he gave it to Colmcille for his first monastery. Though Adomnán mentions Derry many times, he makes no reference to a monastery there, but Manus O'Donnell has such detailed accounts of it from his time, in the sixteenth century, and tradition about it is so strong, that Derry is associated in all our minds with Colmcille.

The word 'Derry' comes from *daire*, the Old Irish word for the oak tree (*doire* in modern Irish). Over a thousand places in

Ireland are called *Doire* or have *doire* as part of their name because of the great oak woods which covered much of the country until a few centuries ago. The oak woods were sacred to the pagan Celts, and the druids (or pagan priests) performed their ceremonies in the sacred groves of oak all over Europe.

Many of the traditions about Colmcille tell of his love for Derry and its oak woods. When Colmcille burnt down the pagan stronghold to clear a space for his Christian church, he took great care to make sure that the woods were safe from the fire. He even built his church in a north-south direction rather than in the usual east-west way in order not to disturb the trees. Colmcille's church was known as DubhRegles and the present Long Tower church is believed to have been built on the same site. Nearby, on the edge of the Bogside, is Saint Columba's Well, covered today by a cast-iron pump and venerated on his feast-day, where legend has it that Colmcille miraculously brought water from a rock to baptise a child.

Colmcille's love for Derry is celebrated in many poems written after his death but attributed to him. So numerous are the angels over that holy place, it says in one such poem, that they stretch for nine waves of the sea around it:

> *They find no room on the land,*
> *For the number of good gentle angels,*
> *Nine waves distant therefrom,*
> *It is thus they reach out from Derry.*

But it was to be another twenty years or so before Colmcille

undertook the journey that brought him to exile on Iona, a tiny island off the west coast of Scotland in the year 563. His life on Iona was to make him famous and his monastery there was to become one of the most remarkable in western Europe, immortalised by Adomnán.

OTHER PLACES ASSOCIATED WITH SAINT COLMCILLE

The years before he left Ireland for Iona were spent in bringing the message of Christ to the people and in founding monasteries. The name of Colmcille is connected with many

places all over Ireland, especially the northern half. When we consider that he left his native land while still in his forties, his personality must have made a great impression everywhere he went in Ireland because there are more legends about him than about any other Irish saint and his name is connected with numerous places where he is believed to have founded churches.

Some of these are in his native Donegal, of course, like Glencolmcille, Tory Island and Raphoe. There can be little doubt about his association with many of these

An ancient cross-pillar in Glencolmcille, Co. Donegal.

sites. The ancient crosses carved on pillars and slabs in Glen-colmcille and in islands off the north-west coast of Donegal, for instance, speak to us from his time. The age-old ritual of doing the *turas* is observed in Glencolmcille and in Gartan probably since his lifetime. Numerous other locations in Ireland revere his memory in the same way. The *turas*, which literally means 'journey', is a widespread and ancient practice all over Ireland whereby pilgrims say prescribed prayers while doing a circuit of what are known as 'stations' at a holy well or other place associated with a saint. Since wells were sacred places to the pagan Celts, these Early Christians were following in the footsteps of their pagan ancestors.

There were also important monasteries at Swords in Dublin and at Moone in County Kildare associated with Colmcille. We find his name as far away as Wexford in Ard Colum and near the river Barrow in County Kilkenny at Kilcolum. A valley deep in the Burren in County Clare is called Glencolmcille and has a medieval ruined church and blessed well. The parish of Colmcille in County Longford takes its name from an ancient ruined church on the island of Inchmore in Lough Gowna believed to have been founded by Colmcille.

Did Colmcille himself really visit all these places? We cannot say for sure, because there are no written records to say that he did, but even if they were founded after his death, like the great monastery at Kells in County Meath, and dedicated to his memory, they are an indication of how famous he was in his lifetime.

CHAPTER FOUR

Colmcille in Legend

Colmcille was a larger-than-life person. He was the kind of person about whom stories get told and retold, with further details being embroidered onto the original story to make it more dramatic and memorable. So it was natural that the Irish people, who were always wonderful storytellers, should tell and retell the legends that grew up around Colmcille.

People sometimes think that legends aren't important because they aren't based on historical fact, but it is often the case that a legend began out of something that really happened. People had a need for heroes in Early Medieval times, just as we do today, and Colmcille was perfect for the role of hero. People love a good story about those who become heroes to them and sometimes it's natural to exaggerate the things they did.

Legends can tell us a lot, too, about the people long ago who told them and listened to them. They needed their saints as special protectors. The dangers of demons, storms, plague and the other destructive powers of nature troubled people greatly, just as they did in the pagan times before Christianity came. In pagan times, people relied on their druids and

magicians to weave spells against these unseen forces, but with the coming of Christianity a man of God with Colmcille's powerful personality was seen as a special kind of protector. He was a good friend to have when things were going badly. God's power was believed to work through him and so people had no trouble in accepting that he could work miracles, even bring the dead to life, for instance. Adomnán, writing soon after Colmcille's death, tells several miracle-stories, as we shall see in a later chapter.

Colmcille's qualities as a protector and as a hero thus give him a special place in the legends and folklore of Ireland. In parts of his native Donegal especially, he is a presence in the community to this day. The name of Colmcille is threaded through sayings and beliefs, blessings and prayers (curses, too); and the right way of doing certain things is the way laid down by Colmcille. When cutting a bank of turf, for instance, you must make sure to leave a ledge half-way down because when Colmcille was being pursued by enemies across a bog in the dark he found himself trapped against a high bank of turf! From then onwards, according to the story, never should a turf-bank be too high to leap up on.

Legends woven around landmarks and natural features in Donegal connect them with the memory of Colmcille, like the little legend that grew up around the stones known as the Stepping Stones, which cross Lough Gartan. In this story Colmcille is taking a shortcut across the lake one day on his way to meet his friends. As soon as he steps into the water, a stone emerges under his foot, and then another and another, so that he is able to walk dry-footed all the way across the lake.

Because he is seen as the hero, Colmcille always comes off best in these legends. Saint Enda of the Aran Islands has a narrow escape at the hands of Colmcille in the following story from Inis Mór. When Colmcille asks Enda for a little patch of his island, Enda refuses because he feels that if he gives Colmcille a foothold in the place at all, the whole island will be called after him for ever because of his fame, his holiness and his noble blood. Enda holds out against all his persuasion until Colmcille finally asks him for a little patch the size of the hood of his cloak. Enda can't refuse him that much, and Colmcille places the hood on the ground, whereupon it begins to spread out in all directions until it covers a whole field – known as Gort a' Chochaill (the field of the hood) to this day. Enda is furious – if he hadn't quickly gathered up the hood it would have covered the whole island and Enda's name would indeed have been forgotten! Not far from Gort a' Chochaill is a little stone altar where Colmcille is still honoured today when the islanders make the ancient 'rounds' of rituals and prayers on his feastday on 9 June.

In the following story Colmcille again comes off best. When he is invited by an angel to build the first church on Tory Island which lies off the north coast of Donegal, three

other holy men go along too, each wanting to be the first. They decide between them that whoever manages to cast his staff all the way from the mainland to Tory will have the honour of being the first saint on the island. They should have known better than to try to outdo Colmcille. His staff becomes a dart when he casts it and it lands on Cruach, while the others all fall into the sea.

COLMCILLE AND MANANNÁN MAC LIR

Colmcille was a great link with the pagan past and some of the legends remind us how the pagan and Christian worlds were connected in the minds of medieval people. The story about his encounter with the great Celtic god of the sea, Mannanán Mac Lir, is an example of this. It is said to have

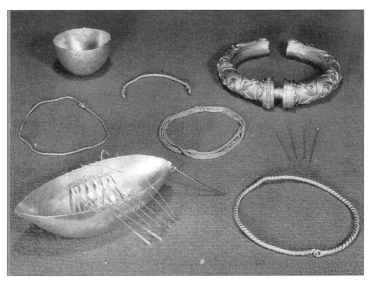

The treasure of a sea-god? This hoard of gold objects was found near Lough Foyle at Broighter, Co. Derry. It may have been an offering to the Celtic sea-god, Mannanán Mac Lir.

happened near Lough Foyle, a place which the Celts believed to be the magical route into the Underworld kingdom of Manannán. Colmcille is praying and meditating alone one day near Lough Foyle when Manannán comes to him walking on the water and engages with him in a kind of contest of magic.

Manannán was a very important god to the Celts. He had the great gift of shape-changing, a fantastic power which intrigued the Celtic imagination: 'there is not a creature from the gnat to the whale that I cannot take on its shape.' Under any of his disguises he could roam the seas, visiting the countries and islands of the 'western', or Atlantic, ocean. Mananán describes to Colmcille the wonders he has seen, the people in strange lands, the wonderful white cattle, the endless droves of sheep. There seems to be nothing on earth that he does not know. Not to be outdone, Colmcille replies that not only does he himself know all that is on earth but all in heaven and hell too, and he pities the great god for his delusions. Manannán is curious to discover what he can about this gap in his knowledge, so Colmcille promises to return on the following day to show him the glories of heaven and the pains of hell. At the meeting-place next day, Colmcille throws his cloak over the head of Manannán, revealing to him dreadful visions of hell, but when this is followed by visions of the delights of heaven, the pagan god is convinced, and is converted on the spot.

In stories such as this the people of medieval Ireland dealt

with the conflict which must still have existed in their minds between the pagan world and the Christian.

COLMCILLE AND THE BARDS

Other legends, like the following one about Colmcille and the bards, show his ingenuity and powers of persuasion with God in a difficult situation. Colmcille encounters a group of bards on the road west of Derry one day. Bards were notorious for their grandeur and self-importance; people had to humour them and give them all the hospitality they asked for, because they dreaded being mocked by them in their poetry. Their satires could bring disgrace on a family for ever for lack of generosity.

This group of bards asks Colmcille to provide them with food and drink here and now. Colmcille wants to show them hospitality in case they ruin his good name, and so he prays to God, 'Since in thine own likeness Thou hast created me, let not shame be put upon that likeness now.' Colmcille goes to a nearby well hoping for a miracle and when he looks in, he finds that God favours him by changing the ordinary well-water into wine in front of his eyes. Not alone that, but Colmcille is directed to a nearby *rath* by an angel, and in the ramparts of the *rath* there are golden goblets for drinking the wine that people buried there long ago. The bards are very impressed and Colmcille's honour is saved. The place came to be known ever afterwards as Rath na Fleidhe (the *rath* of the feastings).

CHAPTER FIVE

Colmcille, the Warrior

THE TURNING-POINT

The turning-point of Colmcille's life came in AD 561 when a great battle was fought at Cúl Dreimhne in Sligo. Then, two years later, in 563, this man who loved his country passionately, who was deeply involved in the life of his tribal family, who was already a living legend everywhere he went, left it all behind to go into exile on the tiny island of Iona off the west coast of Scotland. A whole tangle of legend and historical fact surrounds the battle of Cúl Dreimhne and Colmcille's part in it, and there seems to be no doubt that it was connected to his departure from Ireland.

The famous battle of Cúl Dreimhne is believed to have been the direct result of a serious dispute between Colmcille and the high king, Diarmait Mac Cearbhaill. Colmcille was furious over what he considered to be an unfair judgement which Diarmait made against him at Tara. It all began with Colmcille's love of books. His former teacher, Saint Finnian of Moville, had a copy of the Psalms which interested Colmcille greatly. Finnian had made the long journey to Rome, as many churchmen did in those times, and one of the books he brought back was a copy of a new translation of the Psalms.

This would have been of great interest to Colmcille, and Finnian must have been unwilling to allow him to make a copy of it because Colmcille copied it in secret, having somehow persuaded Finnian to lend it to him, staying up all night several nights in a row to finish it. Making a copy of a manuscript in those times was the only way of having the text and scholars like Colmcille swopped them all the time; also, he saw it as his duty to spread the word of God, so he probably felt very aggrieved at Finnian's lack of generosity and he would have felt justified in secretly copying it.

A little legend in the folklore fills out the bare facts recorded in the annals and puts Finnian in a very bad light. He became anxious about his book and sent one of his monks to recover it. The young monk, rather than ask Colmcille for it , spied through a crack in the door of Colmcille's cell at night and saw what Colmcille was at – busily copying the precious

Ben Bulben in Co. Sligo.
The battle of Cúl Dreimhne was fought in the shadow of this mountain.

book which the whole monastery was talking about. (Another detail of the legend has Colmcille's pet crane, a bird with a long beak, probably what we know as the grey heron, plucking out the eye of the intruder through the crack in the door!)

We can imagine Colmcille's dismay on finding that not alone did Finnian want his book back immediately but that nothing would satisfy him except to get Colmcille's copy of the book as well. Colmcille refused to give up the copy and asked the high king, Diarmait Mac Cearbhaill, who resided in Tara to decide between them. Colmcille defended himself, pointing out to King Diarmait that the book was none the worse for being copied and that it would be wrong of Finnian to keep the word of God from the people. But the high king, to Colmcille's astonishment, decided for Finnian with the famous judgement, the judgement of a king who thinks in agricultural logic: '*Le gach bó a lao agus le gach leabhar a leabhrán*', which translated means 'to every cow its calf and to every book its copy.' Colmcille was outraged by what he felt was a very unfair judgement and though it was against his beliefs as a follower of Christ he was intent on revenge.

Relations must have been at a low ebb between the high king Diarmait and Colmcille by now, but the tragic deaths of two young princes made everything much worse. It happened that Curnan, the son of the king of Connacht was being held hostage in Tara by King Diarmait. Holding of hostages was quite common in ancient Ireland – hostages were usually

Colmcille hastily making a copy of St Finnian's book.

 39

the sons (or sometimes the daughters) of kings and chieftains and they were held to ensure that a territory over which the king ruled was kept in submission; it was like a guarantee of good will on the part of the father of the hostage. But, in a tragic accident, Curnan caused the death of another young prince during a game of hurling. The king of Connacht, fearing for his son, put him under the protection of Colmcille himself, as no king would dare harm anyone under the protection of a holy man. But that didn't stop King Diarmait. Alas for Curnan, he was, in the words of the Annals of the Four Masters, 'put to death by Diarmait, son of Cerbhaill, in violation of the guarantee and protection of Colmcille, having been forcibly torn from his hands.'

The Connacht people were outraged at the execution of the son of the king of Connacht, and for Colmcille the unthinkable had happened. Such an outrage called for vengeance, and in no time he was in the thick of political intrigue like any Celtic warlord. He set out from Tara for Ulster to muster his clansmen, the Northern Uí Néill, who were traditional rivals anyhow of the Southern Uí Néill, to which the high king Diarmait belonged. The high king had tried to stop Colmcille from leaving Tara and had forbidden anyone to go with him. He even tried to ambush him on the way as he travelled over Sliabh Brega in the ancient province of Meath. But Colmcille's great faith in God carried him safely and gave him courage; Manus O'Donnell has him say:

Alone am I on the mountain
O King of Suns, may the way be smooth.

On hearing of Colmcille's complaint, his kinsmen, the Cenél Chonaill and the Cenél Eoghain, prepared for battle and headed south. They joined forces with the King of Connacht and confronted Diarmait, the high king, at Cúl Dreimhne in the Carbury district of present-day county Sligo. That quiet landscape in the shadow of Ben Bulben was the scene of a terrible battle.

THE BATTLE

The high king's army of three thousand men was massacred. By the standards of the day it was a big battle and from the tantalising glimpses we get of it in the annals it was an occasion when the old pagan powers were out in full force. Even though Diarmait, the high king, was a Christian, he must have had a strong attachment to the old pagan ways. His followers fell back on their old druidical ceremonies before the battle, going on a procession 'around the cairns', according to the Annals of the Four Masters. The cairns are probably the tombs in the great passage-grave cemetery at Carrowmore which the high king's army would have passed on their way north to the battle. The tombs are overlooked by the enormous cairn of Miosgán Meadhbha, known as Queen Maeve's Tomb, on top of Knocknarea. They were ancient even then, and would have been the location for pagan ceremonies for generations.

Before the battle began, the high king's druid, Fraochan, made a kind of magical circle or druid's fence, which they called the *airbhi druadh,* between the two armies. He appears to have conjured up a magic mist too to confuse Colmcille's side, as a verse attributed to Colmcille says:

> *O God, wilt thou not drive off the fog which envelops*
> *our number,*
> *The host which deprives us of our livelihood?*

All through the battle, Colmcille stood praying with his arms extended in the form of a cross at the rear of his army. His prayers were answered, the high king's army was slaughtered and only one of his own people was killed, a man who crossed over the *airbhi druadh.*

THE AFTERMATH

Colmcille got back his copy of Finnian's book, but as we shall see, his life was to change forever. As for King Diarmait, his luck seems to have gone against him after the battle of Cúl Dreimhne. He lost another battle the following year; the year after that his son was killed and he was killed himself two years later in 565. After his death, the high kingship went to Colmcille's dynasty, the Northern Uí Néill, and they were to take turns as high kings with the Southern Uí Néill for centuries to come.

The best days of the great royal palace at Tara were numbered. According to tradition it was cursed by Saint Ruadhán

Colmcille prays in cross-vigil before the battle of Cúl Dreimhne.

 43

of Lorrha in Tipperary and after another two centuries or so it fell into decay. Gradually the grass grew over the crumbling ruins of what was once the greatest royal site in Ireland. But Tara continued to fascinate the people of Ireland and it is still regarded as one of the most majestic places of our Celtic past.

CHAPTER SIX

Exile

*In the second year after the battle of Cúl Dreimhne, in
the forty-second year of his age, Columba sailed from
Ireland to Britain, wishing to be a pilgrim for Christ.*

This is a translation of Adomnán's simple description of
Colmcille's departure from Ireland in the year AD 563. The
two events, the battle of Cúl Dreimhne and his exile in Iona,
have been linked together ever since, causing people to be
still intrigued by the connection between them. Was he banished by his fellow saints or did he decide to punish himself
for causing the deaths of so many people? There are mentions
of 'the saints of Ireland murmuring against Colmcille' in dis-
approval of his political involvements. Adomnán even refers
to an excommunication which was immediately withdrawn
due to the pleading of his friend Saint Brendan of Birr. Or did
Colmcille himself think that as a Christian monk he was too
deeply involved in political affairs and conflicts of his kingly
relatives, and thus decide to become an exile as a penance?

It may have been for all these complex and varied rea-
sons, as well as the very simple reason of 'wishing to be a pilgrim for Christ' that Colmcille left the country he loved.

Being 'a pilgrim for Christ' had a special attraction for Irish saints in the early Church. We remember Saint Brendan best for his sea-wanderings, and Colmcille's friend Saint Cormac spent years looking for the most remote place he could find: 'a desert in the trackless sea'.

For Colmcille, leaving his beloved country, his monasteries and his kinsfolk would have been the hardest penance of all. But leave he did, at the age of forty-two at a time when most people of his age were old, if not dead. He had twelve companions with him, all related to him by blood, being members of the Uí Néill clan, and they sailed from Derry, the place he loved best of all.

It must have been a sad leavetaking. By comparison with Adomnán's simple statement, 'in the forty-second year of his age, Columba set sail for Britain', traditional accounts of it are full of drama and colour. The legend which grew up in Gartan tells how Colmcille, the night before his departure, went back to where he was born and spent that lonely night lying on Leac na Cumha (the flagstone of loneliness). To this day, people of this area who have to emigrate come here to pray in the belief that the pain of exile will thus be easier to bear.

The exile of a loved saint was a perfect occasion for highly dramatic accounts, and numerous tales and verses in O'Donnell's Betha commemorate Colmcille's love for Derry and his departure as an unwilling exile, with people weeping and the birds of the air wailing with grief as he sailed away. The stories and verses describe how as Colmcille left Lough Foyle

A sad leave-taking –
Colmcille and his companions sail out through Lough Foyle.

the people of Derry were inconsolable and made the saint's grief all the worse:

> *Since I have heard this lamenting*
> *Why do I still live my days?*
> *The loud wail of the people of Derry,*
> *It hath broken my heart in four fragments.*

According to tradition, he was leaving forever, never again to see the men and women of Ireland, nor to step on Irish soil.

And so, Colmcille 'sailed away from Ireland' in the year 563. The sea was to figure largely in his life from there onwards. His future home, Iona, is a tiny island off the west coast of Scotland. We might well ask why he chose to settle on an island out on the edge of the known world, and how this place could possibly have become such a major centre of culture in the Early Middle Ages. But, in Colmcille's day, of course, the sea could be said to be a means of connecting scattered people rather than separating them. There were constant comings and goings between Scotland and the northern part of Ireland. It was easier to face the open sea by boat than to make your way overland through forests and bogs with the fear of wolves and other dangers threatening. Furthermore, Colmcille was no stranger where he was going and he was to find himself once again in the company of kings and in the thick of politics.

His first port of call was to the great fortress of Dun Add, a hill-fort in Argyll. This stronghold was the power-base of an

Irish settlement in Scotland under their king, Conall Mac-Comhgall. About a century before, these Irish settlers from the Antrim coast, known as the Dal Riada, emigrated to the Argyll area of Scotland from their homeland in north-east Ulster. So there were two sections of Dal Riada, one in Scotland and one in Ireland, both under the rule of the king of Scottish Dal Riada. These Irish were called *Scoti* by writers in the Latin and eventually they were to give their name to the land of Scotland, along with their Gaelic language and culture.

Iona lay on the western edge of the kingdom of Scottish Dal Riada, and King Conall gave permission to Colmcille to found his monastery there. Colmcille was to be deeply involved in the politics of the province as we shall see.

The other people Colmcille was to encounter in Scotland were the Picts, the older pagan inhabitants of Scotland. According to The Venerable Bede, the great English historian, Colmcille 'came to Britain to preach to the northern Picts'. Their king, Brude Mac Maelchon, had his fortress on the eastern side of Scotland near Inverness. He had defeated the Dal Riada Irish in battle a few years before and Colmcille was to make the long journey to his court more than once. Elsewhere on the island of Britain, the Romans, who had occupied the country for centuries, had withdrawn, and a wave of new invaders, the Anglo-Saxons, had poured in and pushed the Celtic people west into Wales and Cornwall.

So Iona was situated in what one writer has described as a sort of inland sea stretching from the Hebrides to the north coast of Ireland, and eventually Iona was to be the head of a *paruchia*, or family of monasteries, stretching from the Orkneys in the far north-east of Scotland to the midlands of Ireland.

CHAPTER SEVEN

Iona

The name Iona is thought to be derived from an Old Irish word *Í* or *Ío* meaning, probably, island. Adomnán, who wrote his Vita in Latin, called it *Ioua insula* (the island of Io) and because at some later date someone misread Ioua for Iona when copying a manuscript, and also because it's easier to say, the name lasted in that form to this day.

For such a tiny island, Iona is a remarkably famous place. It lies west of Argyll in south-west Scotland. If you look at the map of Scotland you see a group of about five hundred islands stretching out into the waters of the Atlantic ocean off the entire length of the west coast. These are the Hebrides and the names of some of them are familiar to us from songs – Skye for instance, and Islay, and the Isle of Mull. Iona belongs to the Inner Hebrides and lies west of Mull. Today, for people who make the long journey overland, Iona is reached by ferry from Fionnphort on the island of Mull, which is only a mile away, across the Sound. In Colmcille's time visitors to the island announced their arrival by shouting across the Sound and then they were ferried across by a boat which hurried to fetch them.

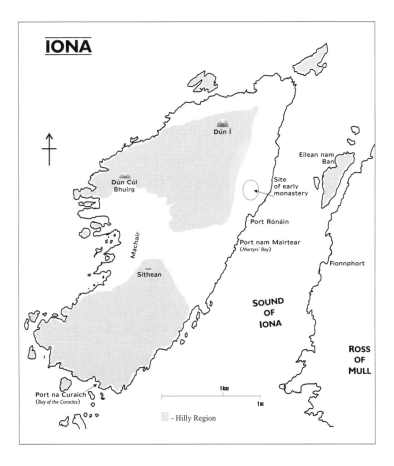

IONA

Dún Í

Eilean nam Ban

Dún Cúl Bhuirg

Site of early monastery

Port Rónáin

Port nam Mairtear
(*Martyrs' Bay*)

Machair

Fionnphort

Síthean

SOUND
OF
IONA

ROSS
OF
MULL

1 km

1 m

Port na Curaich
(*Bay of the Coracles*)

 - Hilly Region

Iona is one of the smaller islands of the Inner Hebrides, being about three miles from north to south and a mile and a half across. It's a gentle landscape for the most part, with beaches of purest white sand breaking the rocky coastline. Colmcille is said to have landed at Port a' Churaich (the bay of the coracles), a pebble beach on the south side of the island.

To the west is the flat grassy plain known as the Machair where sheep graze today and where, in Colmcille's time, the monks tilled their crops. Iona was always referred to by visitors over the centuries as being a fertile place where people

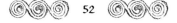 52

were sustained by the produce of the land and of the sea.

North of the Machair, the landscape by contrast is rugged and wild and reaches its highest point at the rocky bulk of the hill known as Dun Í before dropping down again to the sloping farmland of the eastern side where Colmcille chose to establish his monastery and where generations of island people ever since have settled in the precincts of the holy place.

AN ANCIENT PLACE

An island is a wonderful location for exploring the past. We can see the traces of succeeding groups of people as they affected the landscape more easily than we do in other places.

Colmcille and his companions were not the first inhabitants of Iona, by any means, although it may have been uninhabited when they got there. Stone Age people hunted and fished here before 3500 BC and they were followed by early farmers who felled the native elm trees, grazed their cattle and tilled their crops in the open spaces. There were probably periods when Iona was empty of people for centuries at a time. Bronze Age people probably drifted in from Mull, where their standing stones are still to be seen today, but they left little trace of their presence in Iona.

The first clear signs of human settlements in Iona date from around the first century BC. Then, on the rugged northern part of the island, the Celtic people of the Iron Age made their home. On the top of Dún Cúl Bhuirg, a rocky hill on the northern edge of the Machair, are the remains of a rude fort they built with a

sturdy stone wall for shelter and a hut inside with a hearth in the centre. Archaeologists found that these Celtic people used pottery, and that someone among them had owned yellow glass beads, perhaps strung together as a bracelet.

We might wonder what ceremonies they performed here in this craggy place overlooking the wild and rugged landscape north of the Machair. It's in startling contrast to the gentle, even levels to the east, on the far side of these hills, which Colmcille and his pioneering Christian monks chose for their settlement. We don't know whether these pagan folk were still on Iona when Colmcille and his companions arrived, but we have another reminder of the pagan tradition in the hill known as Dún Mhanannáin, named after Manannán Mac Lir, the god of the sea. Another connection with the pagan past was at the hill named Síthean Mór, visible across the Machair from Dún Cúl Bhuirg, where an ancient ceremony of racing horses in the direction of the sun on Michaelmas Day lasted until a few centuries ago. As so often happens, the pagan and the Christian traditions merged in this place, and another name for the same hill is Cnoc na nAingeal (the hill of the angels) where legend tells us that Colmcille was visited by a heavenly vision of angels. Today, the 150 or so inhabitants of the island live in the cluster of houses on the sheltered eastern side of the island where Colmcille chose to settle, with a jetty at Saint Ronan's Bay. From here the modern ferry from Fionnphort plies to and fro, making the same journey as Colmcille's companions made in the days when the monks

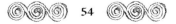

rowed back and forth in their currachs.

But everyone is drawn, naturally, to the most prominent building on the island which is the medieval abbey. It dates from about AD 1200 and it stands within what remains today of the *vallum* or monastic enclosure (you can see the course of the *vallum* in the aerial photograph on page 57). This is the old earth-and-stone bank which enclosed the Early Christian monastery later than Colmcille's time, and somewhere on this same site, he first established his community in their wattle buildings.

The events of the centuries in between have wiped out all traces of the early monastery of Colmcille. The wooden buildings may have been sturdily built, but were worn out by

A beach in Iona with Dún Cúl Bhuirg in the background.

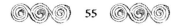

weather or burnt down by fires, and they would have been replaced repeatedly. Archaeologists have returned again and again to Iona and made special studies of the area where the first monastery grew up. Their findings have given us a lot of information about life in the early monastery.

Adomnán's Vita too, though its main purpose was to tell us about the saintliness of Colmcille, is full of information about the monastery, the buildings it contained and the life the monks lived there under their abbot, Colmcille.

We believe that Colmcille's settlement was in the southern part of this area and surrounded by a sturdy enclosure which probably had bushes growing on top, giving good shelter and a look of importance to the settlement. This enclosure corresponded to the ringforts they all knew so well in Ireland and it served the same purpose. Indeed, Colmcille was a bit like a chieftain in the way he ruled his community, keeping in touch with all his farflung interests.

The monks may have been attracted to this spot because of the oak and ash trees that grew there, providing convenient building materials. The trees were quickly used up and wood had to be brought from the mainland in later times. Very few trees grow on Iona today. Holly grew here too, and was probably used for making ink for the writing of manuscripts.

There were several buildings within the enclosure, as each monk probably had a sleeping-hut or cell (*cubicula*). The monks would have put all their skills to work in those early

Iona from the air, showing the restored medieval monastery. You can see faint traces of the vallum *in the foreground. Somewhere to the right of the monastery was the site of Colmcille's first foundation.*

days, collecting wattles, weaving them into sturdy panels for walls, covering them with thick mud to keep the draughts out and then thatching the roofs with reeds. They would have had no windows, but Colmcille's own sleeping-house had a half-door – the kind that lets in the light like a window when you open the top half. Colmcille himself slept on the floor of bare rock and according to tradition had a rock for a pillow. The other monks were only slightly more comfortable on beds of straw.

Colmcille spent much of his time in another hut known as the *tegorium*, which had a wooden floor and was built on top of the rocky mound known as Tórr an Aba. This was where

he wrote, received guests and oversaw the workings of his monastery. He was always accompanied by his attendant Diarmait, who was a relation and who outlived him by many years. There was a special house for guests (*hospitium*), and a communal building which housed the kitchen and refectory – this was probably where the monks sometimes sat in the rare times when they weren't hard at work. Probably only the raging storms of winter confined them indoors.

All these buildings were scattered around an open space called the *plateola*, which the monks crossed on their way to the church. Colmcille and his monks would have built the church in the rectangular shape introduced into Ireland with Christianity and they probably decided to use oak planks rather than wattle for this, the most important building in the monastery.

We know that it had a small annex to the side called the *exedra*, and perhaps this was used for the safe-keeping of precious objects like altar-vessels and special books. The beautifully-carved high crosses were erected in the eighth century, long after Colmcille's time, but we know that the monks erected wooden crosses in the early days.

I O N A, THE HOME OF D I Y

The monastery must have been a hive of industry. Colmcille's monks had all the skills for making everything that was needed by the community. Fortunately, they swept the debris of their various trades into the ditch outside the enclosure,

The community at Iona.

thus giving archaeologists plenty of information about their daily lives. Someone took charge of the tannery where they made leather from the skins of the cattle and sheep. Skins and leather, especially the skins of cattle, were put to all sorts of uses, from covering boats to making vellum for the manuscripts.

Sheepskins were used as containers for carrying milk when people were going on journeys. Satchels for storing and carrying books in were made of leather. Shoes were cut out of leather and stitched, and decorated with little punched holes. Several of them have been found and they are in the style of the shoes we see in illustrations of monks in manuscripts.

Other monks knew about iron-working, and they would have made the knives and other tools needed around the farm and the workshops. The monks were also expert at woodworking. They liked to use alder for vessels that would have a lot of wear, and these they turned on a lathe. They worked vast amounts of timber on Iona over the years. As time went on they had to import oak and pine from the mainland, a difficult and dangerous operation. Adomnán describes how in his own time, having dragged the timbers laboriously across the land, they used currachs to tow huge beams to Iona for the renovation of the buildings and again for the building of a longship. Building a longship – an ocean-going vessel like the Scandinavian warships – would have been a major undertaking and would have required great expertise. Later still, in the eighth century, great

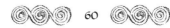

blocks of stone were brought by sea for the carving of the high crosses. The currachs used for this difficult task were rowed with bladed oars but they also carried a mast, and we know from Adomnán that the monks' work was made easier when they got favourable winds, and they always used sails when the winds were right.

FARMING ON IONA

Like the workshops, the farm was central to keeping the monastery self-sufficient. The acres of tillage on the Machair (the western plain) kept the community supplied with enough grain for bread all year round.

The farming-monks would have walked the mile or so every day on the winding track through Gleann an Teampaill between the low hills to the open spaces of the Machair. It must have been a pleasant place to work when the sun was shining, being so close to the sparkling sea, with cool breezes blowing from the west, but like all farming people, they were at the mercy of the weather. A wet spring, for instance, or a drought, meant a late start for the crops and a poorer harvest. But the harvest was usually good on Iona and a barn full of grain in the autumn, blessed by Colmcille, was their reward.

Though they had horses on Iona we know from Adomnán that the monks carried the corn home themselves to the barn which stood outside the enclosure. Meanwhile, there were the cows, the calves, the sheep and pigs to be attended to in the pasture. The monks hunted for deer on Mull and on the

mainland, and they went on special expeditions to the nearby island of Erraid to catch seals. The seals were probably useful for their oil, for burning in lamps.

WORK AND PRAYER

It was a life of relentless hard work and prayer. Prayer and their devotion to God under the authority of their beloved abbot, Colmcille, united the monks in all their varied tasks. From sunrise to sunset the day was measured by the call to prayers every three hours. As well as that, the bell was struck again at midnight and the monks hurried across the courtyard, with their lamps, to chant the midnight office.

The bell was the means of calling the community together from their diverse tasks, of communicating news and of summoning them to prayer. Sometimes in the middle of the night if Colmcille had reason to call for urgent prayers he would cry out, 'Strike the bell', and the community would hurry to join him in the church.

Such was the environment in which Colmcille lived and worked, the world of an Early Christian monastery.

The monks carry the harvest of barley home from the Machair.

CHAPTER EIGHT

Man of Prayer, Man of Action

MIRACLE-WORKER

We get the impression from Adomnán that Colmcille was a man of boundless energy, a spiritual leader and a brilliant organiser who was always available to his community. In appearance he is believed to have been very tall, and his voice was remarkable for its carrying power. He must have been physically strong and rugged when we consider all the difficult journeys he made even in his later years and the fact that he was at work right up to his death at the age of seventy-six, a great age in those times. Like the rest of the monks, he would have worn his hair in the style of tonsure of the Irish Church, shaved straight across the front of the head from ear to ear. Dressed in the garb of the Irish people of his day, he wore the *brat* (a woollen cloak) and the *léine* (a linen ankle-length tunic, usually white) of the time.

He was never idle. We can visualise him in his wooden hut on top of Tórr an Aba, the faithful Diarmait posted at the door ready to carry out any instructions, every moment of his day filled with the endless tasks involved in running an important monastery, as well as writing, copying manuscripts,

planning his long journeys, receiving guests who brought news from home and keeping in touch with his far-flung monasteries. He also fasted and spent long hours in vigil.

The Vita is full of stories of the everyday events of Colmcille's life in the monastery and of the loving concern he showed for the monks in his community. His kindly nature went out to them and revived their spirits when they were tired and weary from work. Adomnán relates how, as they walked home exhausted in the evenings from the Machair, a journey of over a mile, carrying their heavy loads, they experienced a renewal of their energy in the very same place each evening and felt a sweetness in the air which took all their tiredness away. They were sure it was caused by Colmcille's spirit coming to meet them on the way to make their journey easier.

Colmcille often wept with sorrow on hearing bad news or when his special insight showed him something which was happening far away. He was most upset when his monks in Durrow, in the distant midlands of Ireland, were worn out from working on a new building in the monastery. Their abbot, Laisran, gave them no respite from work and they were exhausted. But it was as if in some way Laisran was touched by the sorrow of Colmcille because at that very same time he ordered the tired workers to stop for food and rest and he decided not to make them work any more that day or on any day when the weather was bad.

As Colmcille sat writing in his cell, he was in touch with all

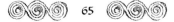

the comings and goings of the monks and they never passed by without getting his blessing on their work or on their implements.

Most of all, these little stories show us the preoccupations of medieval people with things like demons, the dangers of the sea, death.

Demons were something you had to guard against at all times and the blessing of a holy man like Colmcille kept them in their place. Demons lurked in the bottom of milk-pails, people believed, just as they did in pagan times, and the sign of the cross before milking made sure they were kept away. A boy called Colman forgot this simple precaution one evening before milking the cows, and as he passed Colmcille's hut on the way home with his pail of milk he stopped as he usually did for a blessing. As soon as Colmcille gave his blessing on the milk-pail, the lid was flung off and thrown to the ground and most of the milk was spilt. This was said to be caused by a demon in the milk-pail who became agitated under the power of Colmcille's blessing and took flight.

Angels are also a constant presence in the stories about Colmcille. They struggled with the demons and defeated them, they escorted the souls of good people to Paradise when they died and they kept Colmcille company while he was praying and contemplating. They sometimes went to help his friends when he was too far away to help them himself. Colmcille was distraught when he had a vision one day of a young monk in his monastery in Durrow falling from the top of a high building. But even as he fell, Colmcille's wish was said to have sent an angel speeding from Iona to save him before he touched the ground.

DANGERS AT SEA

People were always coming and going in boats. (Saint Brendan too, the great explorer, was Colmcille's friend and visited Iona.) But the sea held many terrors even for those people who, like the community of Iona, were seasoned sailors. It represented all the mystery and dread of the unknown, and people needed their saints to call on God to protect them. God, they believed, worked His miracles through powerful saints like Colmcille, so it was quite normal to expect that they could even have control over the weather. With the wrong winds people could be blown off-course and become the prey of the monsters that lived in the sea and be lost for ever.

The holy man, Cormac, had a narrow escape on one of his voyages when the south wind blew. It was a good wind for sailing north from Ireland to Iona, of course, but Cormac was a restless wanderer. He set off farther north from Iona in search of 'a desert in the trackless sea', some island remote enough to be a hermitage. It was summer-time and the wind blew non-stop for fourteen days and nights during which time Cormac and his companions were driven further north than anyone they knew had ever been before. They must have been feeling hungry and lost. Worst of all, they were

terrified by hordes of sea-monsters, tiny creatures which surrounded their boat and threatened to puncture its skin sides. They prayed with all their might for a change in the wind.

At that very same time, Adomnán tells us, Colmcille, far away in Iona, knew of the urgency of their need and saw the great danger they were in. He lost no time in bringing the community together with the sound of the bell and they prayed to God, in tears, for a change in the wind. All of a sudden, the wind turned around to the north and, to the immense relief of the poor lost sailors, the boat could go south again and before many days they made it to Iona safely.

Adomnán also tells the story of two holy men, Baithene and Colman, who were both sailing off from Iona in different directions, Baithene north to the island of Tiree, Colman south to Ireland. They both came to Colmcille to ask for his prayers for favourable winds, and, just as he hoped, Baithene got the south wind so he could make his journey under full sail to Tiree. Later the same day, Colmcille, knowing that Baithene had landed safely, sent for Colman and told him to set sail for Ireland as the wind was about to change to a northerly breeze. Colman and his companions also got home safely on that same day, their journey made easier in the belief that they were under God's protection due to the prayers of Colmcille.

Guests were an important part of life on Iona. Isolated as they were as an island community, news of the outside world was always of great interest and importance. Colmcille met sailors from Gaul on the mainland who brought news of a terrible volcano in Italy which killed thousands of people. Visitors would bring letters from sister-monasteries at home and from kings and abbots looking for Colmcille's advice, perhaps, or inviting him to make a visit home in order to attend an important meeting.

All kinds of people found their way to Iona: saints and founders of monasteries like Saint Brendan of Clonfert, who is known for his great voyages, and foreign sailors blown ashore by shipwrecks. Sinners came as well. Some, hoping to mend their ways, were sent to an island which was known in Colmcille's time as Hinba. Scholars have decided that Hinba must be the island of Canna which is near Skye. It was a place where Colmcille founded another monastery where he often went to pray and where people went to do penance.

One guest who received special attention was a bird known as the crane, probably the bird we know as the grey heron. Colmcille announced one day that he was expecting an exhausted crane to arrive shortly on Iona from Ireland and he asked one of the monks to wait for him on the shore

The wind-blown crane was tenderly cared for by the monks.

and to get ready the guest-house. When the poor storm-battered bird fell onto the shore he was carried to the guest-house and tenderly cared for for three days. Then after gathering strength he took to the sky and flew home to Ireland.

Colmcille seems to have had a great affection for the crane (he is depicted in another story as having a pet crane, you may recall). Could it be because the crane was believed to possess the secret alphabet of knowledge in pagan times, and that Colmcille with his love of knowledge was devoted to it for that reason?

CHAPTER NINE

Colmcille and the Picts

Colmcille had to leave his beloved island many times and make long journeys as a missionary and as a diplomat. Some of his most important journeys were to the kingdom of the Picts.

His first journey there would have been to establish his claim to Iona and to gain the confidence of the Pictish king, Brude Mac Maelchon. Other journeys in Pictland were to demand all his experience as a diplomat and as a warrior-saint.

Relations were always delicate between the Picts and the people of Dal Riada in which Iona lay. Only a few years before, the Pictish king had defeated Conall, king of Dal Riada, in battle. Colmcille, being a prince himself, was an ideal go-between and he helped to keep the peace between them. It was his intention, too, to convert the Picts to Christianity, but even though he made a great impression on their king, Brude Mac Maelchon, Brude was to remain a pagan.

The Picts were the oldest inhabitants of northern Britain. The Roman soldiers used to call them *Picti*, which means 'the painted ones' from their habit of painting or tatooing their bodies. Like the Irish, they had never been subdued by the

Romans. Pictland stretched away to the north as far as the Orkneys. The Roman poet Calgacus called the Picts

the most distant men on earth,
the last of the free.

They were sheltered by their very remoteness. They were made up of many scattered tribes, and the great rugged mountains and glens of the north made it easy for them to escape from pursuers. Centuries before, the Roman general Agricola thought seriously of invading Ireland from the coast of Scotland, but his experiences with the Picts probably persuaded him to give up the idea. The Romans made much

of the one victory they had over the tribes of the north at Mons Grampius, and they sailed all around the coast of Scotland in a show of bravado – but they never got a foothold in the country.

The Picts had no knowledge of writing so we know very little about

Pictish art: a serpent, an abstract Z-rod and a mirror are incised on this Pictish symbol stone.

them apart from what others tell us. Their language was a form of Celtic, and we can see traces of it in place-names that begin with the element Pit- (which means 'share'), as in Pit-caple (share of the horse), and Pitlochry (share of the stones). But they are best known for their remarkable art. Their carved symbol-stones are unique and beautiful and their

Dating from Christian times, a beautifully carved cross stands out against a backdrop of twining animals on this Pictish cross-slab at Aberlemno.

strange patterns may have been the same as those they painted on their bodies. They were wonderful craftsmen. The stone carvings show birds such as eagles and geese, and there are horses, wolves and serpents and fish. There are mirrors and combs with abstract designs like zig-zags. All these objects must have had a special meaning for the Picts. There were hundreds of carved stones standing in the landscape, perhaps at special meeting-places or on boundaries of land. Other carvings appear on stone plaques and were built into the walls of fortresses like the magnificent bulls from the fortress at Burghead.

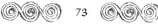

The Picts learned how to make Ogham inscriptions from the Irish and carved them alongside their own symbols. As time went on and they became Christianised, they carved magnificent cross-slabs with intricate designs. Their craftsmen travelled too, taking their ideas with them, and eventually we see their influence on the wonderful high crosses in Iona and even in Ireland.

They used silver which they probably stole from the Romans for making beautiful objects like heavy chains and brooches. These chains were probably worn by kings. King Brude could well have worn a chain in the way that other kings wore crowns.

Brude must have been a formidable king to confront in his fortress. He had been on the throne since the year 555 and reigned for thirty-three years. His father, Maelchon, is thought to have been a Celtic prince from Wales who married a Pictish queen. The Pictish throne, we believe, was matrilinear; thus kings were chosen from the mother's line. Still, Colmcille and Brude did not share a common language; we know from Adomnán that they spoke through an interpreter.

To reach the court of the Pictish king, Colmcille and his companions had to make a long and hazardous journey to the other side of Scotland. King Brude had his court in the great fortress of Craig Phádraig. It was a huge hill-fort with timber ramparts near present-day Inverness, and here Colmcille was to find himself back in the old pagan world of druids, spells and magic.

 74

Their journey brought them across 'the spine of Britain', as Adomnán called the great mountain mass of the Grampians. Fortunately their way was made easier by the fact that they could cover much of the journey by boat through the Great Glen which slices its way through the mountains. They would have sailed up Loch Linnhe and Lough Ness, where they were to encounter the famous monster, and carried their boat over the rugged ground when they had to go on foot. They spent the nights camping by streams. They had some narrow escapes. One night their boat would have been lost in a fire if Colmcille hadn't sent someone to save it just in time – he knew that they were being followed by an enemy. The whole village behind them where they had left their boat was devastated by the fire.

The visit to Brude got off to a bad start. When Colmcille and his companions arrived at the gate of the fortress, Brude, we are told, acted haughtily and kept the doors shut against them.

But when Colmcille made the sign of the cross on the doors, the bolts slid back and the doors opened before him. Brude was alarmed at the power of his guest and hurried to meet him and welcome him with honour. Ever afterwards, he showed Colmcille great courtesy and, though not a Christian himself, he paved the way for the future work of Colmcille and those who came after him.

But Colmcille had the pagan forces to contend with still. A very important member of Brude's household was his foster-father, Broichan the druid.

Many people think that this Broichan is none other than the druid Fraochan, the weaver of magic spells who had been part of the court of Diarmait Mac Cearbhaill, the high king at Tara. He would have remembered Colmcille very well from the battle of Cúl Dreimhne – it was he who had made the 'druid's fence' for the high king's army a few years before when Colmcille's prayers had helped defeat them. You remember that Colmcille's clan, the Northern Uí Néill, won the high kingship as a result of that battle, so Broichan probably felt it was time to try his fortunes elsewhere. He may well have left Ireland after that defeat, under a slight change of name, and gone to Wales which was home to many druids. There he could have met the young prince, Brude, who became his foster-son; then he went with Brude to the Pictish court on his marriage. He must have been dismayed to be confronted once more by such a formidable adversary as Colmcille.

According to Adomnán, the druid did his best to outdo Colmcille with his magic spells and they had several confrontations, but Colmcille's miracles won the day and gained him the respect of Brude, the pagan king. In fact, some of the most remarkable of Colmcille's miracles are recorded in connection with his journeys among the Picts. He is said to have

brought a young man back to life one day. This young man's family had been converted to the Christian faith on hearing Colmcille preach, and when their son became ill and was in danger of death, the druids mocked the grieving family, belittling the Christian God they believed in. Colmcille arrived as the young man was being buried. He prayed alone over the corpse and God restored the man to life, confounding the druids and their arrogance.

The druid Broichan himself came off worst in another wonder-working contest with the saint. Briochan kept an Irish slave-girl in his household whom Colmcille wanted released. When the druid refused, Colmcille promised that unless she was released, Broichan himself would die. Colmcille lost no time in carrying out his threat. The glass the druid was drinking from shattered in his hand as he was struck down by a violent seizure, and in no time he was at death's door. Colmcille was down at the river Ness, and knowing that it was a life-or-death situation for the druid, he waited for the inevitable call for help. When two men on horse-back arrived with a message from the king, asking Colmcille to restore the health of the dying druid, Colmcille sent two of his own people to the king with a stone from the river and the uncompromising message that if Broichan released the slave-girl, then dipped the stone in water and drank the water, he would live. 'But if he refuses,' the message went, 'he will immediately die.'

The slave-girl was released, the druid drank the water and was instantly restored to health. The king kept that stone

among his treasures for the rest of his life to cure people who were sick, and the strange thing was that whenever it was put in water to invoke the blessing of Colmcille, it floated on top like an apple or a nut.

But the druid remained his mortal enemy. On the day when Colmcille was leaving Brude's fortress for home, Broichan stirred up a magic mist on Lough Ness and caused a storm to blow just as Colmcille was setting sail. But Colmcille, praying to God to be on his side, set off bravely in front of the watching crowds and through his prayers the winds turned around and the mists fell away.

THE MONSTER

Colmcille is the first recorded person to have had a brush with the dreaded water-beast that we know as the Lough Ness monster. It is said that he even managed to strike terror into that mysterious creature.

The story goes that he saw a young man being buried one day on the bank of the river Ness. He had been bitten by the monster while swimming and he was dead when his friends dragged his body ashore. Colmcille ordered one of his companions, Lugne, to swim across the river to bring back a boat from the other side. That brave young man leapt straight into the water and no sooner had he reached the middle of the river than the monster, having tasted blood, swam to the surface and with a roar that terrified all the onlookers, he rushed towards the unfortunate Lugne with gaping jaws. But

 78

The Lough Ness monster in full retreat from Colmcille.

Colmcille made the sign of the cross in the air and commanded the monster to return to the depths. The beast, terrified, disappeared into the depths as if pulled by ropes, causing the pagan onlookers to be amazed by the power of the Christian God.

Colmcille may have not been the first to bring Christianity to the Picts, but his journeys in Pictland established friendly relations with them and marked the real beginning of their conversion to Christianity.

CHAPTER TEN

Colmcille, the Scribe

Colmcille was a famous scribe in his day. Adomnán's Vita is full of references to his love of books, his constant reading, his writing in manuscripts, his copying of the Psalms. It really upset him if someone spilt ink or dropped a book on the ground. In pagan times no-one could read or write, but the Christian message was a religion of the book, so with the coming of Christianity, as we have seen, monastic schools had to be set up, Latin had to be learned, manuscripts had to be copied. Indeed, the knowledge in books gave rise to a whole new art-form, as Irish monks were to become some of the greatest scribes and painters of books in the world. And as Colmcille himself was one of the most important of them, we must look now at the story of how the Irish style of writing grew from very small beginnings into what was to become the 'book hand' of Western Europe for centuries to come.

Few manuscripts survive from Early Christian times, particularly before AD 700 and those that are still in existence remind us sadly of all that must have been lost. These few books show us how writing developed in Ireland in its early days, from the century before Colmcille's time until it

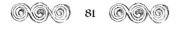

reached its most glorious expression in the Book of Kells.

To begin with, there are the Springmount Bog Tablets, as they are known, in the National Museum of Ireland. Named after the bog where they were found in County Antrim in the early twentieth century, these are six oblong wooden plates with holes bored through them so that they would have been bound together to make a book of wooden leaves. The interior of each plate is hollowed out and filled with wax, to give a good surface for writing on with a pointed object like a stylus. Scholars who have made out the text recognise it as being a particular version of the Psalms from around AD 400. The writing itself, too, is seen to be very early in form and it could well be the kind used at the time of the arrival of Saint Patrick.

The first actual manuscript we must look at is the Cathach – and there is good reason to believe that this is from the hand of Colmcille himself. He would have written or copied dozens of books of course, but the Cathach is the only surviving one that could have possibly been written by him. Tradition has it that this is the very book that he copied from Saint Finnian's manuscript, giving rise to the battle of Cúl Dreimhne which caused his exile.

Scholars who have examined the script believe it is actually old enough to have been written by Colmcille. Like many of our great manuscripts, the Cathach had many adventures before it reached its present home in the Royal Irish Academy in Dublin. The word Cathach means 'battler', and during the Middle Ages the O'Donnell clan to whom it belonged always

[Folio image of the Cathach manuscript with Latin text in insular script]

A page from the Cathach. (Folio 21 r)

brought it into battle with them, where it was carried three times around the troops in order to ensure victory – the

O'Donnells were the main branch of the Cenél Chonaill, Colmcille's own tribe. In the eleventh century, it was put into a special wooden box covered with metal in the Columban monastery in Kells for Cathbharr O'Donnell, chief of the

The initial letter D from the Cathach. This manuscript is believed to have been penned by Colmcille himself. (Folio 19 r)

O'Donnell clan, so it was always closely connected with Colmcille.

The manuscript itself is a copy of the Psalms. Only fifty-eight leaves survive and at first sight it may seem to appear very simple and unadorned, by comparison with the

A carved piece of antler from the fifth or sixth century from Dooey, Co. Donegal.

special feature of the Book of Kells; when this scribe took up his pen to write the initial letter D, he drew it in the ornamental style of the pagan art which he was used to seeing on brooches and pins and other ornamental objects. The spirals, the little trumpets, the tiny triangles around the capitals, were all familiar to the eyes of Colmcille and so he translated them onto the page. These little decorative features are found in one form or another in manuscripts in Ireland and Britain for centuries afterwards.

A penannular brooch dating from the sixth or seventh century. The curvilinear style of art on this object was current in Ireland in the lifetime of Colmcille.

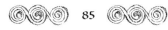

Scribes were at this stage beginning to use colour on the pages, and the capital letters in the Cathach were painted, probably in yellow, with most of the larger capitals surrounded by red dots.

These developments in writing were uniquely Irish, as was the way in which the letters decrease gradually in size after the initial letter. This technique is known as *diminuendo* (diminishing) and is a lovely way of linking the big capital to the rest of the text, giving balance and liveliness.

The actual script, or the way in which the letters are formed in the Cathach is called Irish majuscule, and this is the very script that Colmcille used when copying his manuscripts or when teaching his scholars to write on their wax tablets. It was practised on Iona and from there it was later transplanted to Lindisfarne, where there was a famous scriptorium, so that a great extended family of manuscripts in Ireland and Britain grew from the very pen of Colmcille himself.

The Book of Durrow is another manuscript closely associated with the *'familia'* of Colmcille, where you can see the development of the Irish script and of manuscript illumination. The Book of Durrow was written about seventy years after the death of Colmcille, probably in Durrow itself.

About a thousand years later, after Henry the Eighth had dissolved the monasteries, this book was kept by a farmer near Durrow who used to cure sick cattle by giving them water to drink into which he had dipped the book – even then

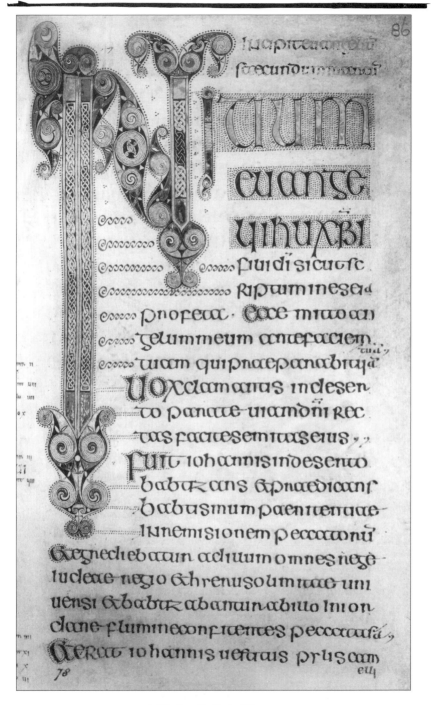

A folio from the Book of Durrow.

Colmcille's connection with books was seen to be miraculous. It was rescued in the seventeenth century by an officer in Cromwell's army called Henry Jones, who later became Vice-Chancellor of Trinity College in Dublin and presented it to the college where you can see it today.

The Book of Durrow is a copy of the Gospels, written in beautiful majuscule. The pages are elaborate and colourful by comparison with the those of the Cathach. The initial letters have become extremely important. The IN of the word *Initium* is a good example of this, running almost the length of the page and filled with spirals and interlace. Whole pages are given over to colourful designs painted in green, yellow and red – these are known as 'carpet pages'. Another page has strange animals which the scribes must have seen on Anglo-Saxon ornaments, chasing each other around the borders of the page. It is a book of great beauty and gives us a foretaste of how the art of book-illumination was to reach its greatest magnificence in the Book of Kells.

The Book of Kells, one of the most beautiful and famous manuscripts of all time, was closely connected with Colmcille and his community, though made long after his death. Its earliest history has caused great controversy, but many people believe that the Book of Kells, 'the Great Gospel of Colmcille' as it is called in the Annals of Ulster, was begun in Iona as a way of celebrating the two hundredth anniversary of the death of their founder. In what better way could the memory of Colmcille be honoured by his monks than by

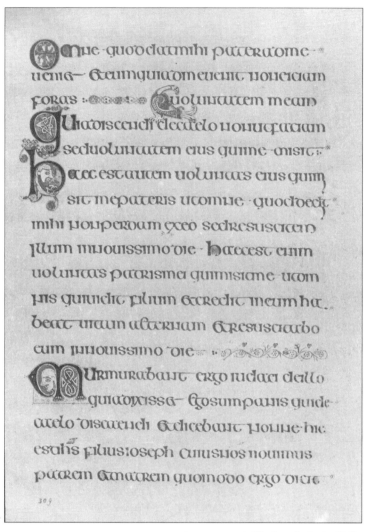

A folio from the Book of Kells.

lavishing all their skills as scribes and as painters on a magnificent copy of the Gospels, the Word of God? But the Viking raids began on Iona before it was finished, making life there precarious, as we shall see, so the monks brought the Great

Book with them in its unfinished state to their new monastery at Kells in Ireland, where it was completed (in fact, it was never really finished).

It must have taken years to write. Three painters, at least, worked on it and at least three different scribes wrote the text. It is a truly magnificent book. There are full-page portraits of Christ, of the Evangelists, and of the Virgin Mary painted in lavish colours. Cats, mice, dogs, geese and numerous other birds and animals run and play through the text to amuse us. Animals, angels and men in contorted shapes curl around themselves to form letters. The scribes used all kinds of playful devices. Little animals or birds point the way to the next word when a line of text ends in the line above it. The scribes called this device *'cor fa casan'* (turn-in-the-path) or *'ceann fa eite'* (head-under-the-wing). The Book of Kells is endlessly fascinating, a work of real genius.

Giraldus Cambrensis, who visited Ireland in the twelfth century, was so enthralled by the beauty of a great book he saw in Kildare that it must have been the Book of Kells he was describing when he wrote: 'You will make out intricacies, so delicate and subtle, so exact and compact, so full of knots and links, with colours so fresh and vivid that you might say that all this was the work of an angel and not of a man.'

Monasteries, then, and especially those in the *'familia'* of Colmcille, were homes to immensely talented people, where creativity and works of the imagination that can still fill us with wonder today, were encouraged and nurtured.

One manuscript which definitely was written on Iona still survives today. This is a copy of Adomnán's Life of Columba, written by the scribe Dorbhene, an abbot of Iona who died in 713. It is one of the finest Irish manuscripts and the most important account of all of life in an Early Christian monastery. Luckily it was brought intact to Germany during the Viking invasions and is now in a library in Switzerland. (You can see a reproduction of a page from this manuscript on the first page of this book.)

Iona is believed to have been the first monastery to begin writing the annals. What are the annals? Monasteries in the early Church began to keep records because they had to calculate the date on which the important feast of Easter fell each year. This was very complicated to do, and had to be written down as it was different for every year. (The question of when the great feast of Easter should be observed was the cause of a bitter controversy during the centuries after Colmcille's death.) At the same time, it became a custom to write down any major event that affected the life of the monastery, like the death of an abbot, or unusual weather-conditions or battles in which they had an interest – just a line for each event. The monks of Iona were very careful about keeping records, and though it's no longer in existence, the Iona Chronicle, as it is known, was the most important of these earliest records. Though it was lost long ago, it was like an ancestor to the other annals such as the Annals of Ulster and another set of annals known as the Annals of Tighearnach.

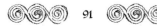

The Iona Chronicle was probably begun in Colmcille's time (certainly during the abbacy of Adomnán) and brought to Ireland for safe-keeping around 740, probably to the monastery at Bangor in County Down, where it was copied into other sets of annals, like the Annals of Ulster. The Annals of Ulster are the most complete and the most reliable of all the Irish annals. The earliest copy is lost, like so much else, but they were copied into several later manuscripts; the best one is in a fifteenth-century manuscript in Trinity College in Dublin. You can see a modern printed edition of the Annals of Ulster in most public libraries today, a twentieth-century offshoot of the earliest literary activity on Iona.

The Annals of Tighearnach, like the Annals of Ulster, were descended from the Iona Chronicle (Tighearnach, the scribe, was a monk in Clonmacnoise). The Annals of Ulster and of Tighearnach together tell us a great part of the story of early historical times in Ireland and in Pictland, as they are 'descended' from the Iona Chronicle.

BOOKS AS RELICS

Many beautiful legends surround Colmcille's love of books, and, as we have seen, people believed that books written by his hand had miraculous powers. Many stories tell how books written by him survived all kinds of catastrophies.

A little legend from Gartan tells how a copy of the Psalms which Colmcille left all night on a rock in Gartan was protected by a dove who covered it with her wings. The book

 92

was found safe and sound in the morning. The rock is pointed out to this day on the roadside in Gartan.

Then, Adomnán tells us of the unfortunate young man who fell into the river Boyne carrying a satchel of books and who was not found for twenty days. All the books were destroyed except for a page 'written by the holy fingers of Saint Columba' which was found as dry and perfect as the day it had been written.

After his death, Colmcille's books were treated as relics by the community of Iona. In times of drought, they carried his books around the western plain while they prayed for rain to make the crops grow. It is said that he never failed them. In time they also adopted the habit of laying his books and clothes on the altar while they prayed before some special undertaking like a hazardous journey by sea with a precious cargo of timber for the building of a new church.

CHAPTER ELEVEN

Colmcille, the Kingmaker

We get an idea of the stature of Colmcille when we see his involvement in the crowning of Aidan, the king of Dal Riada. Conall, the king who had given Colmcille the island of Iona, died in 574 and a new king had to be chosen. Just as in Ireland, the kingship did not pass from father to son, kings being chosen by the tribe, and on this occasion Colmcille had the final say in choosing the next king of Scottish Dal Riada.

It must have been a very difficult decision for him. The choice was between Conall's two nephews, Iogenan and Aidan, and Adomnán tells us that Colmcille would have preferred Iogenan. He was a gentle person and had the respect and love of Colmcille, but Colmcille could see that Aidan was a powerful warrior and had the makings of a stronger king. Colmcille was not a man to shrink from a tough political decision. Aidan had enemies of course, as he was already known as an ambitious warrior, and there was strong opposition to him. But Colmcille recognised that he had the qualities that were needed to unite the people of Dal Riada into a strong and powerful kingdom. He decided for Aidan after spending days and nights praying in solitude on the island of Hinba.

Colmcille's word decided it and Aidan came to Iona itself to be crowned.

This decision of Colmcille's was backed up, he believed, by order of God himself. According to Adomnán, an angel appeared to him during his vigil on Hinba and gave him a book of glass in which were written the names of all the Dal Riada kings, with Aidan's name next on the list. When Colmcille was still showing signs of reluctance to select Aidan as king, the angel struck him a dreadful blow with a scourge and threatened him with further visitations unless he chose him. (Colmcille was known to have carried a livid scar on his body until the day he died, but many people have wondered whether this was a relic of his warlike past, rather than the result of his encounter with an angel.) Colmcille finally decided for Aidan and he was to become the greatest of the kings of Dal Riada, with Iona under his protection.

The fact that a king should be chosen by a holy man of lesser rank than a pope, and ordained by him, was unheard of in the early Church and shows the strength and authority of the first abbot of Iona.

A VISIT HOME

Colmcille's next excursion into politics called for a visit home to Ireland. Some of the most well-known legends about Colmcille tell how he came back to Ireland to the Convention of Druim Ceatt blindfolded and with sods of turf tied to his shoes because of his promise never to see Ireland again or to

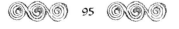

set foot on Irish soil. Whatever about the legends, Colmcille made more than one visit to Ireland and he was a formidable presence at a great convention of kings which took place at Druim Ceatt in 574 near present-day Limavaddy in County Derry. Colmcille was there to make sure that good decisions were made. It was a very important meeting, a bit like one of the big summit-meetings of today.

The meeting was held to spell out the relationship between Scottish Dal Riada and its territory in Ireland. One of the most important things to be discussed was whether the people of the Irish territory of Dal Riada should continue to be subject to the Dal Riada king in Scotland or should owe their allegiance to the king of the Northern Uí Néill.

The central person at the convention was Colmcille – he must have been seen as a sort of senior statesman by now. He had led his kinsfolk, the Northern Uí Néill, to victory at Cúl Dreimhne, breaking the power of the high king and his pagan court. He had strengthened the kingdom of Scottish Dal Riada and he had befriended and won the respect of the formidable Pictish king, Brude Mac Maelchon, paving the way for good relations between the Pictish kingdom and the kingdom of Dal Riada. His mission at this great convention at Druim Ceatt was as adviser to Aidan, king of Scottish Dal Riada, whom he had crowned the previous year in Iona.

Another king present was Colmcille's first cousin, Aed Mac Ainmire, king of the Northern Uí Néill who was later to become high king of Ireland. So Colmcille had strong

connections with both sides and an agreement which pleased everyone was reached. It was decided that the men of Irish Dal Riada were to do military service for the Uí Néill overlords but that the king of Scottish Dal Riada was to get their taxes and tributes. This gave great recognition to the kingdom of Scottish Dal Riada and the outcome was very important for Iona, ensuring as it did, the continued friendship of King Aidan.

THE BARDS

There was another important question to be decided at Druim Ceatt. The bards of Ireland were falling out of favour with the people, as we have seen already. Times had changed in Ireland during the previous hundred years. People were less dependent on the bards than they used to be. Not long before, they had been among the only educated people in Irish life, a privileged class, but Christianity brought literacy and new beliefs and people had less time for the old traditions. People disapproved of the bards' connections with druidism too, rooted in paganism as it was.

But the bards weren't willing to give up their status. They tried to convince themselves that nothing had changed and that they were as powerful as ever. They became ever more demanding, and, as the traditional stories tell us, they exploited people's generosity shamelessly, travelling around the country with huge retinues and being a terrible nuisance.

By the time of the Convention of Druim Ceatt, the bards

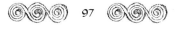

were in danger of being expelled from the country, but according to tradition, Colmcille himself spoke eloquently in their favour. Colmcille realised that if the bards were banished it would mean the loss of a great ancient tradition of learning. He managed to persuade the assembly to reach an agreement with them and they were saved from banishment on condition that they reduced their retinues and limited their powers. Tradition tells us that the bards, hundreds of them, rose to their feet to sing the praises of the wise man who had championed them.

And real evidence for the way Colmcille was regarded in his own time is in a famous poem called 'Amra Choluimb Chille'. Composed by one of the chief bards immediately after Colmcille's death, it demonstrates the respect shown to him by this ancient and learned class of people. It was written as a special farewell to Colmcille by Dallán Forgaill, who understood Christian learning but had been educated in the traditional bardic way. This very difficult poem is a work of extravagant praise for Colmcille, in which we hear of his holiness, his goodness and his learning.

'THE PILLAR OF MANY CHURCHES'

But Colmcille's real role in life was that of a holy man, a revered abbot and a founder of monasteries. It was on one of his visits home to Ireland that he founded one of the monasteries he loved best, that at Durrow in present-day County Offaly. A long time before, he had been given a gift of the land for a

monastery here at Dairmhagh (Durrow) which means 'the plain of the oak-trees' and there may have been a small community of monks there before the main monastery was established around 585.

This monastery is most famous for one of the great gospel-books to which it gave its name, the Book of Durrow, which was written in the century after Colmcille's death. From Durrow, Colmcille visited the famous monastery of Clonmacnoise on the Shannon. The two places were linked by the great route known as Eiscir Riada which linked east and west in Early Christian Ireland.

In Scotland, he travelled far and wide baptising people and spreading the word of God. According to the Venerable Bede, numerous monasteries in Scotland were founded by Colmcille and the monks of Iona. Adomnán tells of his visits to the Isle of Skye, and of his many journeys through the

A ninth-century high cross at Durrow, Co. Offaly.

Ardnamurchan district of Scotland. He was constantly visiting his monasteries in the nearby islands of Tiree and Hinba, and one known as Cella Diuni near Lough Awe.

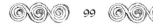

CHAPTER TWELVE

Saying Farewell

More than thirty years had passed since Colmcille first left Ireland. He often thought of his final home in heaven and he began to wish for the day when he could go there. Colmcille's last days were filled with this joyful expectation and he spoke of the angels who were waiting to escort him to Paradise. The monks were often sad when they knew he was getting ready to leave them, and after Easter in the year 597 he began to say farewell to Iona and to his community, doing the rounds of his duties as a loving abbot. He was an old man by now, seventy-six years of age, very old indeed by the standards of the time, but his unquenchable spirit and love of living never left him. He allowed himself to be carried in the monastery's horse-drawn wagon to visit the western plain for the last time. The farming-monks were at work there and he gave them his blessing, and then he blessed Iona and the inhabitants of the island.

On his last day, which was a Sunday, he said his farewells. He visited the barn with his attendant, Diarmait, to bless the great heaps of grain, and he praised the monks for their harvest of the previous autumn.

It was then that he revealed to Diarmait that he was going to leave them at midnight 'to go the way of the fathers'. Diarmait was overcome with loneliness and sadness and Colmcille tried to console him as well as he could. On his way back to the monastery, he sat down to rest. As he sat there, the old white horse which used to work on the farm came up to him, and, sensing that his beloved master was about to depart forever, he mourned and wept bitterly. Diarmait wanted to send him away but Colmcille understood the grief of the poor sad animal and blessed him for the last time. (After his death, that place where he rested on his way back from the barn was marked by a cross fixed in a millstone, and it was still standing when Adomnán was abbot a century later.) Then he climbed the little hill known as Cnoc nan Carnan which overlooked the monastery and gave his blessing to the holy place, saying that the day would come when it would be honoured as a place of pilgrimage of saints and kings. He went to his hut then and spent some time transcribing a book of Psalms. He stopped at the thirty-third Psalm where it says, 'But they that seek the Lord shall not want for anything that is good.' He left the rest for his successor, Baithene, also a scribe and a teacher, to finish.

It was time then for vespers, the evening office in the church, and afterwards he went to his sleeping-hut, where, according to Adomnán, he reclined on his bed of rock with a stone for a pillow – this same stone for many years afterwards stood beside the grave of Colmcille as a memorial. He gave

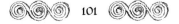

his final messages to Diarmait to deliver to his community, urging them to live in peace with each other and promising to be always ready to intercede for them with God.

When the bell sounded for the midnight office, Colmcille rose from his bed and hurried to the church ahead of the rest of the monks where he sank to his knees to pray before the altar. Diarmait, who was first into the church after him, related afterwards how the whole church was filled with an angelic light which faded as the others approached. It was Diarmait who found Colmcille lying at the altar. He raised him up and rested his head on his lap, and when the rest of the monks arrived with their lights a moment later, they all began to lament as they could see that their beloved saint was dying. Colmcille gazed around once with a look of deep happiness and Diarmaid raised Colmcille's arm so that his right hand could give his final blessing to the community. Colmcille, Columba, the Dove of the Church was dead.

The spirit of Colmcille lived on, and his work, begun in Iona, continued to flourish after his death. The abbots continued to be learned men, all relatives of Colmcille, making Iona famous as a centre of culture and learning. Adomnán, who became abbot in 679, was himself a renowned scholar. His Vita Columbae (Life of Columba), tells us more than any other book about life in an Early Christian monastery.

While Adomnán was abbot, the sea continued to cast up all kinds of visitors to the island. When a raging storm caused Arculf, a Gaulish bishop, to be shipwrecked off the western coast of Britain, he made his way to Iona, having heard of Adomnán's reputation as a scholar. There he spent many hours telling Adomnán about his travels in the Holy Land, and about the people and the cities of the Near East. Adomnán wrote it all down on waxed tablets and it became De Locis Sanctis, an early travel-book about the holy places in the seventh century.

The sea also brought the young prince Oswald, an exiled prince of Northumbria in the north-east of England, and he spent part of his exile in Iona where he became converted to

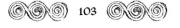

Christianity and learned to speak the Irish language while in hiding from his father's enemies. When he became king of Northumbria, he sent to Iona for help in converting his people, and in 636, the monk Aidan left Iona and founded a monastery in Lindisfarne (holy island), a tidal island off the coast of Northumbria. Aidan and his monks travelled the length and breadth of Northumbria, preaching and baptising.

This led to the founding of other monasteries, to the spread of learning and the writing of beautiful manuscripts like the Lindisfarne Gospels. Scribes in the new monasteries learned to write in the Irish majuscule and this is the script which at this stage we call 'insular' because it has become the book-hand of the islands of Ireland and Britain.

But there were dark days ahead for Iona. The sea, always such a powerful presence, brought danger too. In 795, the Vikings struck for the first time. In 802, the Annals of Ulster announce: 'Í Coluim Chille was burned by the heathens'; in 806: 'the community of Í, to the number of sixty-eight, was killed by the heathens'. In 807, because of the danger of further attacks, a new monastery was begun at Kells in County Westmeath and some the community moved there. They brought with them the Book of Kells, 'the great Gospel Book of Colm Cille' which was begun on Iona but finished at Kells as we have seen.

Iona was plundered again in 825. This time, the raiders were looking for the precious shrine containing the relics of Colmcille. It was the practice in Early Christian times to

enshrine the bones and other relics of holy founders in containers covered with precious metals like gold and silver. Rather than give it up, Blathmac, the abbot, hid it under a layer of turf and was killed with his companions, but the shrine was recovered by the monks who survived the slaughter. Later on, the relics were divided; some were brought to Ireland and others given to the king of Dal Riada. In the year 849 Kenneth Mac Ailpin, king of Dal Riada, became king of the Pictish throne as well, and he founded a dynasty which was to unite a Scottish nation where the culture and language were Gaelic.

The magnetism of Iona as a holy place continued to draw people there. Two Irish kings were buried there in the late eighth century. In 980, the King of the Norsemen in Dublin, Olaf Cuarán, went 'in penitence and pilgrimage' to Iona, where he died. The kings of Scotland down to the eleventh century are said to be buried there, though not a trace of their graves is to be seen today. Around 1200, a Benedictine monastery was founded on Iona, replacing the old Irish foundation. It flourished until about 1560, when the destruction caused by the Reformation left the buildings derelict. Even after that, the tranquility and beauty of Iona continued to attract a growing number of travellers, including Samuel Johnson, Sir Walter Scott, William Wordsworth, John Keats, Robert Louis Stevenson, Felix Mendelssohn.

Today, the abbey buildings have been restored and are in the care of the Iona community, and modern pilgrims come

here to withdraw from the world for a while and to experience the peace and beauty which are the legacy of Colmcille's island home.

Colmcille was an innovator who welcomed change. Ireland must have been in the throes of cultural upheaval in his youth. It went from being a society with a largely illiterate ruling class to a country which was to create new horizons in learning and the arts. The changes brought by the book-learning which came with Christianity must have been like the revolution brought by the information technology of today.

But Colmcille and others like him 'moved with the times' as we say today. He was a leader who brought the country out of centuries of isolation. He became a priest himself, and probably the fact that he belonged to a ruling dynasty gave strength and acceptability to the new religion and the learning that came with it.

Colmcille had time for the past as well; he was a powerful character who governed his monasteries like a chieftain, in the way of his ancestors, the way he knew best. Perhaps this was a factor in the phenomenal contribution made by Irish scholars to European civilization, making Ireland truly an 'island of saints and scholars'.

BIBLIOGRAPHY

Lives of Colmcille

Anderson, A.O. and M.O. (eds), *Adomnán's Life of Columba*, (Edinburgh, 1961)

O'Donnell, Manus (ed. A. O'Kelleher and G. Schoeperle), *Betha Colaim Cille*, (Illinois, 1918)

Reeves, W., *The Life of St. Columba written by Adomnán*, (Dublin, 1857)

History of Early Ireland and Early Scotland

Byrne, F.J., *Irish Kings and Highkings*, (London, 1973)

Mac Airt, S., and Mac Niocaill, S., (eds), *The Annals of Ulster*, (Dublin, 1983)

Smyth, A. P., *Warlords and Holy Men: Scotland AD 80--1000*, (Edinburgh, 1984)

Sutherland, E., *In Search of the Picts*, (London, 1994)

Early Monasticism and Way Of Life in Early Christian Ireland

dePaor, M. and L., *Early Christian Ireland*, (London, 1958, repr. 1978)

Herbert, M., *Iona, Kells and Derry: The History and Hagiography of the Monastic Familia of Columba*, (Oxford, 1988)

Herity, M., *Studies in the Layout, Buildings and Art in Stone of Early Irish Monasteries*, (London, 1995)

Horn, W., White Marshall, J., and Rourke, G., *The Forgotten Pilgrimage of Skellig Michael*, (University of California Press, 1990)

Hughes, K., and Hamlin, A., *The Modern Traveller to the Early Irish Church*, (London, 1977)

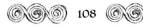

Donegal and Derry

Lacy, B., et al, *Archaeological Survey of County Donegal*, (Lifford, 1983)

Lacy, B., *Siege City; The Story of Derry and Londonderry*, (Belfast, 1990)

Nolan, W., Ronayne, M., and Dunlevy, M., *Donegal: History and Society*, (Dublin, 1995)

Tunney, J., *Saint Colmcille and the Columban Heritage*, (Donegal, 1987)

Iona

Clancy, T.O., and Márkus, G., *Iona: The Earliest Poetry of a Celtic Monastery*, (Edinburgh, 1995)

MacArthur, E.M., *Columba's Island: Iona from Past to Present*, (Edinburgh, 1995)

MacArthur, E.M., *That Illustrious Island: Iona through Traveller's Eyes*, (Iona, 1991)

McNeill, F.M., *An Iona Anthology*, (Iona, 1990)

Royal Commission on Ancient and Historical Monuments of Scotland (RCAHMS), *Argyll: An Inventory of the Monuments, vol. 4: Iona*, (Edinburgh, 1982)

Art of the Period

Henry, F., *Irish Art in the Early Christian Period to AD 800*, (London, 1965)

Henry, F. (ed.), *The Book of Kells*, (London, 1974)

Meehan, B., *The Book of Kells*, (London, 1994)

Ritchie, A., *The Picts*, (Edinburgh, 1989)

Youngs, S., *The Work of Angels*, (London, 1989)

Other books by
THE O'BRIEN PRESS

The World of Colmcille is part of a series of books for both adults and children telling of Ireland's ancient past in uncomplicated prose and lively, beautiful presentation. Illustrated with specially commissioned reconstruction drawings, and photos of remains, artefacts and sites relating to each topic. The other books are listed below.

EXPLORING THE BOOK OF KELLS
George Otto Simms
Illustrated by David Rooney

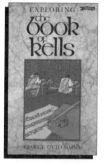

A compact guide to both the content and the making of this outstanding world treasure by a world renowned authority. Illustrated in colour and black and white, with reproductions from the Book of Kells.   Hardback £7.99/€10.15/$11.95

BRENDAN THE NAVIGATOR
George Otto Simms
Illustrated by David Rooney

The famous medieval adventure story of the sea voyages of Brendan, who is said to have visited America long before Columbus. Illustrated with pencil drawings.

Paperback £4.50/€5.71/$7.95

THE REAL STORY OF PATRICK
Who Became Ireland's Patron Saint
George Otto Simms
Illustrated by David Rooney

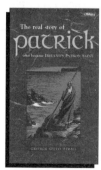

The unique life of Ireland's patron saint as he himself told it in his Confessions, and the legends surrounding him.   Paperback £5.50/€6.98/$8.95

THE VIKINGS IN IRELAND
Morgan Llywelyn

Illustrated by David Rooney

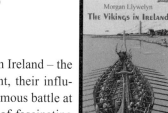

The complete story of the Vikings in Ireland – the earliest raids, the gradual settlement, their influence on Irish art and on trade, the famous battle at Clontarf, their lasting legacy. Full of fascinating detail.   Hardback £7.99/€10.15/$12.95

EXPLORING NEWGRANGE
Liam Mac Uistin

The creation, building and discovery of Newgrange, a stunning megalithic tomb in County Meath that is older than the Egyptian pyramids. Its man-made celestial calendar still keeps perfect time after 5,000 years.

Hardback £7.99/€10.15/$12.95

POCKET SERIES

A POCKET HISTORY OF IRELAND
Breandán Ó hEithir

Concise, insightful overview of Ireland's history from Celtic times to the present, including the North of Ireland.

Paperback £4.99/€6.34/$7.95

A POCKET HISTORY OF ULSTER
Brian Barton

Unravels the complicated origins of the northern state and of the religious divide, and tells of the development of the state up to modern times. *Illustrated with photos.*   Paperback £5.99/€7.61/$8.95

A POCKET HISTORY OF THE IRA
Brendan O'Brien

An accessible, clearly written account of the IRA from its beginnings to today. Covers the origins of the movement, its aims, its political and military thinking, and the major personalities who have shaped its development over the years. *Illustrated with photos.*

Paperback £4.99/€6.34/$7.95

A POCKET HISTORY OF IRISH LITERATURE
A. Norman Jeffares

Traces the long and noble list of Irish poets, dramatists, novelists and short story writers from Swift to the late twentieth century. Includes all the well-known writers and places them in context with their lesser-known compatriots at the period of their writing. *Illustrated with photos.* Paperback £4.99/€6.34/$7.95

A POCKET HISTORY OF GAELIC CULTURE
Alan Titley

Gaelic culture is famous all over the world – but what is it? This book is an engaging view of the story of music, language and the arts in Ireland from prehistory to the present day. Paperback £4.99/€6.34/$7.95

A POCKET HISTORY OF IRISH REBELS
Morgan Llywelyn

The stirring story of eighteen of Ireland's greatest rebels, from the sixteenth century to today. The personalities featured include Grace O'Malley, Theobald Wolfe Tone, Daniel O'Connell, Countess Markievicz, Patrick Pearse and Michael Collins. Paperback £4.99/€6.34/$7.95

Send for our full colour catalogue